Kellie Lee currently resides in Australia. After ignoring her unique experiences and gifts throughout her life, fearing judgement, she fully stepped onto her spiritual path several years ago to 'live from her true authentic self' and start to serve her purpose for this world. Being guided, she sold her home, changed her life, career and embraced her gifts. She is now an international personal development coach and mentor, soul practitioner, energy healer, intuitive psychic and medium. She has coached people from all around the world in all areas of her expertise, and walks her path by her intuition and universal guidance daily.

For You... My One...

Kellie Lee

FLYING WITHOUT WINGS

AUSTIN MACAULEY PUBLISHERS™

LONDON • CAMBRIDGE • NEW YORK • SHARJAH

Ordering Information:
Quantity sales: special discounts are available on quantity purchases by corporations, associations, and others. For details, contact the publisher at the address below.

Publisher's Cataloging-in-Publication data
Lee, Kellie
Flying Without Wings

ISBN 9781641829656 (Paperback)
ISBN 9781641829663 (Hardback)
ISBN 9781641829670 (E-Book)

The main category of the book: Biography & Autobiography / General

www.austinmacauley.com/us

First Published (2019)
Austin Macauley Publishers LLC
40 Wall Street, 28th Floor
New York, NY 10005
USA

mail-usa@austinmacauley.com
+1 (646) 5125767

Dear Reader,

I am honored you have picked up my book *Flying Without Wings* to take this journey with me. My purpose in sharing with you my raw truth, my vulnerability, along with my beautiful love and energy experiences, is to help you reflect upon your life, your choices, in the hope to create a better life for yourself. Also, to understand in every moment, the power of love and the power of energy. There are many messages and insights in this book for all ages. I ask one thing of you. When you have finished my book, please hold on to it, of course share with others if you feel drawn too, but keep my book on your shelf or close by so that as you come across those difficult decisions and times in your life, you can refer back to the part or parts in this book that most resonated and that you know will help you. Also, from a place of knowing, you are never alone.

–   Kellie lee

Prologue

Have you ever felt like you had a destiny that you had no idea what it was but knew you were here for something in particular.

This story may appear quite unusual in nature for some, however, it will resonate with those who feel they have lived an unusual life, and those who felt they never really fitted in, or still don't.

On my journey through life, I thought my situation was rare. While following my path and sharing with others my extraordinary truth, which manifested into reality, I realized as rare as it may seem, there were others in this world of ours who were also having unique experiences.

Knowing that something or someone is missing, never feeling whole or complete, that missing piece we try to fill with so many other things as we travel through life, but nothing ever quite fits the same as your perfect match.

This is my incredible story that led me to the most profound love and connection of human existence, plus as I was to discover on a soul energetic level of existence. Let it be known, 'The Soul' is our most powerful connecting life source. When you have finished this journey with me, which I promise you will enjoy, you will never look at life the same way. It will help you to understand the depth and level of just how energy is everything, and how it can manifest itself in every form.

...from a little girl until now, let me share something so sacred with you all that will inevitably light the fire within.

Chapter 1
The Beginning

I was born in the beautiful city of Melbourne, Australia – with its stunning old buildings, iconic Flinders street clock tower, traditional trams ushering up and down our wide-open streets, our diverse culture, stunning street lights, and lush gardens – all which makes this city one of the most picturesque cities in the world. In lots of ways, it feels like a 'mini' London, not anywhere as big of course, but the style and architecture similar. I love this city, still, with all my heart, and therefore it remains high on my list as one of my favorite cities today. In the center of the city, *at this time,* stood an old stunning building built in 1896 of deep red brick with cream trim. This building became famously known as the 'Queen Victoria Hospital' – and this is where I took my first breath.

My mother's family were city people and back then could be declared as quite financially fortunate, so it was expected I would be birthed at one of the best facilities. However, the city wasn't for my mother so it was inevitable that we would move. Her lifetime desire to live by the beach was destined to become her reality, and when I was three years old she encouraged my father to do just that. We decided to pack up and move 'our family' – my father, mother, brother, and Sailor (our very clever Border collie canine) – to a small coastal town by the water known to many as 'The Peninsula'. We resided by this Peninsula which was 90 minutes south of the city, for many years, enjoying the lifestyle and making it our home.

Around this time, the world was experiencing the spiritual revolution, the sexual revolution, psychedelic drugs to enhance people's consciousness, expressing love, feeling peace, and living in harmony. It was the 'Age of Aquarius' shown to us through the hippie movement. But I'm not quite sure how much of that filtered down to where I lived in Australia. It was also a time of the Vietnam War, but thankfully my father was a little too old to go.

So here I was born into Generation X, the forgotten and silent generation, where our first view between the spiritual movement and war reflected a contrast of good and evil. It was a time of growing up without a large adult presence since both parents worked, and it was the beginning of independence plus liberation for women, which was a good thing. However, this led to our generation having to become more independent and self-sufficient, trying to find our own way in the world, resulting in us becoming more addicted to peer orientation. It's quite interesting we were also known as the generation that never grew up, but yet became the first gen that had to mature and grow up fast. We partied like no generations before us with a new sense of freedom. We worked hard and played hard and were the first to journey into clubbing, excessive alcohol drinking, drugs and more. To describe these decades using the terms sex, drugs, and rock and roll isn't far wrong. Sadly, though, we didn't seem to set a good example for our future generations. In saying that, in these decades, we entered into this more for the element of fun, having a great time feeling wild and free, not so much for a place to escape our worries and depression.

One could say I was lucky to experience this time, or one might say we were the unfortunate generation, but either way I was here, so I had no choice. I will say one thing though, growing up in the '70s and '80s was a trip, and over those two decades our generation appeared to have experienced the most changes in this world than any other generation before us. However, mine had a bit more of a twist.

From as early as I can remember, and even earlier that which my mother can recall, I had an imaginary friend. My special 'invisible friend' that came with me everywhere, and I couldn't do without. It was like the two of us came as a package, or at least it felt that way, and my family saw this as well by knowing in every situation that Kellie was with her invisible friend. It was just the regular normal thing at home with them commenting in passing, "Oh she is talking to her friend again", and it was never really discussed in a negative way. My friend was so vivid, illuminating, and rich in light, our conversations so expressive, and I thought my situation was normal in this world. I thought every child had one; I didn't see it as being rare at all because it didn't seem that uncommon for little children to have imaginary friends. We often hear about this, and we also often get to witness as these innocent children speak to their imaginary friends like they exist. Some can see them, most chatter away to them having full conversations like I was, all whilst not bothering at all what others think. Why do we not worry about what others think? That would be because it was just normal to us. Maybe certain young children can see something we all can't; *do we ever stop to think that 'maybe they can'?*

It's often talked about how children can see spirits at an early age, and they can also sometimes feel an energy presence. They also feel extremely natural and comfortable talking to their imaginary friends, but most times adults think the child is pretending, so they don't ask the child exactly what they are experiencing. (No one ever asked me). The more I got to think about this; I conclude it's a silly observation that adults would think this. Because at such a young age, children have not been subjected to any human 'conditioning' from this world at this point. Their little minds are not clouded with ego debris; they wouldn't know to make it up or much less need to. They are just open little loving ones simply seeing and saying it how it is – being truthful.

Young children are innocent, only knowing unconditional love and happiness, along with simplicity. In terms of life, we can learn a lot from them. Some do stay awakened to this as they grow up, but mostly we all fall unconscious to this when little and lose our higher awareness – *this wasn't the case for me.*

My recollection is from about three years old, but according to my family I used to talk to my imaginary friend as soon as I could speak. A beautiful energy or presence was what it felt like, that radiated such pure love and was with me constantly. In every way, it felt like it was a part of me, and I wondered if everyone else had an energy friend in their life. I wondered: *Was this how it worked? Was this really what everyone felt on earth?* It must be, because I felt more connected to this energy than connected to this life. As bizarre as that sounds, it was very much the truth. Everywhere I went my friend was with me, at home, outside, or if I traveled to other places. It didn't matter where I was, they were with me. We used to talk, laugh, have fun, play together, and I would love sitting on the end of my bed talking to them. We had conversations about everyday things, what we wanted to do, where we wanted to go play, and what things they wanted to show me. And in all this time, my energy friend exuded an incredible protection for me that felt natural in every way, and made me feel extremely safe. I felt, *at this early age*, they were directing or guiding me, and I could see far beyond my world I was living in. This was 'normal' for me – my every day. And my mother, father, and brother fully accepted this was with me, it was never questioned – they accepted I had this friend.

Mum would say in a loving voice (with no judgment) "Who are you talking to, love, is that your friend?" And I would reply,

"Yes, Mum."

I felt totally at ease expressing my true self, together with the recognition to all about my friend. Maybe having such an accepting and understanding family helped, or maybe I would have been myself anyway, I couldn't be too sure, but to me, it felt normal to do so, for how else could I express my authentic self – who I really was – if I never included the very part I felt so bonded to? I knew my mother couldn't feel or see my friend. She probably thought, at times, she had some weird child talking to herself. However, she could see they were very much real and special to me, and I was never teased or judged, just accepted. I think parents of children back then who had imaginary friends probably questioned silently if the child could see a spirit that they couldn't. I'm sure it was also an era when none of them would openly confess that, but today, it's possibly a different story.

When meal times rolled around, I would set an extra place at the table next to me for my friend, it was expected because this is how it worked, or if anyone else set the table they knew to set a place as well. No one was allowed to sit there since that spot was always reserved for my friend and everyone knew. We were always together, and I was always acknowledging them, it was no secret – I was never alone.

However, in myself, I felt different from everyone else, and being so young meant I wasn't able to describe exactly how I felt. Looking back now, I can explain it as if I felt I was 'living between two worlds'. I was living in a world that didn't feel right to me, but yet with my invisible friend by my side I felt I could make it work. Why was *I* different though? *Why me?*

Over time, I suppose I looked different to others and many people became curious asking me, "Who are you talking to?" when I was conversing or playing with my friend. They would ask with a little smile on their face along with a giggle as if they were laughing at me, and 'again' I would simply tell them, "My friend." At this age, I didn't know they were laughing at me I thought they were laughing with me, the fun I was having and how happy I was. It would be some time before I realized what people were really thinking.

I think those who have never had an experience like this before think we are a bit crazy. Crazy because it's unknown to them, also it's something they can't see. Perhaps, in some cases they may also think we are feeling incredibly alone as children, and we need to invent a friend to be with. This wasn't the case for me, I loved playing with my brother, and we had other children around, plus, I was happy at home with my family, I didn't need to invent a friend. My energy friend was very much here, I never knew any different, they were the closest to me in every way and felt like home to me.

As time moved on, and I had aged a little, people said things to me about my friend in a condescending tone. As they asked questions or sometimes they just looked, I would look up to see the smiles on their faces, and I started to feel 'from their energy' that they were not smiles from love, not smiles from wanting to know or try to understand my experience I was having, nor were they open to the possibility and belief my friend was real, and it did start to hurt me. Sometimes, it made me feel I was silly or stupid, and I knew I wasn't but still, it wasn't very nice at all. I myself could feel energy well, and I just knew in their energy that they were mocking me, thinking I was weird or strange. The one thing that confused me that I didn't understand was why they couldn't see or feel energy like

14

I could, but it became quite obvious to me they couldn't, and because of this I just knew most couldn't feel what I felt; I knew on every level they didn't understand.

Had I transitioned into this world carrying an understanding of life beyond this physical plane, an existence not known to others? Were there more souls out there like me? Feeling old but yet a child... And if there were, I wondered if they all had energy friends like me.

"Old souls are said to be a special kind of person, they usually feel from birth that they don't fit in, feeling isolated and alone. Deep within their hearts they feel old in every way, in mind, body and soul. They see themselves as different and tend to live their life more internally, feeling others don't understand them.

This could very well explain that, perhaps, I wasn't strange after all; perhaps, I was very much an old soul – That Remembered!

Chapter 2
Who Am I?

Well, I obviously was a very old soul. But at three, four, or five years of age, I had no idea about that. I just knew I felt different and very lost. However, this incredible universe blessed me with the most amazing soul to be my mother.

She was an attractive lady of above average height, a brunette but had birthed two children as fair as could be. Her curly short waves fell soft around her face and her smile lit up any room. When she spoke, her sweet voice brought a sense of calmness to all, a vibration of peace that rippled beyond. She was like a beautiful radiant shining star whose light shone so bright around others, and she was so loved by all. I never saw my mother judge, gossip, or degrade another human being; she had the presence of an angel and oozed unconditional love. If someone needed help, my mother was always there for everyone. Her love, strength, and compassion were shown consistently to all, while her energy was soothing to be around.

I would say the only characteristic that was my mother's defeat at times was that she always put others before herself, one I inevitably inherited that took me many years to change. Of course it's beautiful to help and serve others, as we all should, but not sacrificing to the detriment of ourselves.

Along with Mum, I was blessed with my father; he was a gorgeous man. He was tall, dark, with a strong physique, and the looks of a movie star. Of course, being his daughter, I was biased. But throughout his life, people often commented on how similar he looked to the actor, Rory Calhoun. He was an extremely hard worker with a passion for life and never judged or entered into anyone else's business either. He always accepted people for who they were and allowed them to be themselves. Quiet, with a soft calming nature he was, until you pushed his buttons. It took a lot but when you did it was time to start running.

My brother, well I hit the jackpot with him as well; I couldn't have wished for a better soul as a brother. I know we all say that, but truly, he was amazing, and we shared a bond as siblings. He had fair blonde hair with blue eyes, was cute as a button (like me), and loved music. Being Passionate about music would be an understatement, as early as he could talk he would be saying 'Muuusick', and in fact I think the first word he ever spoke was 'Music'. Being the big brother, he did what big brothers are supposed to do, protect their little sisters along with loving them without judgment, and he certainly did this. He was older than me by four years, and I was most grateful. It was nice having an older brother that could watch out for me, and even with our age difference he was always interested in us doing things together, never treating me like a 'nuisance' little sister, like some brothers do.

Our beautiful black and white Border collie 'Sailor' was also part of our family. Sailor was a very smart dog that had joined us before I was born. He was one of us, and we would take him everywhere, *well wherever we could,* and although originally he was bought as my brother's dog, we all shared him equally.

In addition to Sailor, we had a rather large sleek pussy cat. He was the color of ginger and walked with the confidence of a tiger but possessed the most gorgeous timid nature. Like Sailor, he was very friendly and loving with our family, always wanting cuddles and to sit on your lap or the sofa curled up beside you. Along with them both, we also had seven chickens taking up residence in our backyard, one of which had taken a shine to me. She was the cutest little chicken, and I was happy watching her run around from a distance, but she had other ideas. As soon as she was roaming free and spotted me, she would run towards me wanting to be held or sit on my lap, she never did it to anyone else, just me. I may have spoiled her in the beginning a little by playing with her and then that was it, she never left me alone. It was cute though, she loved me and to her I was her best friend. Because of this, she became my unusual pet, and I was usually nominated for the daily fresh egg collections.

So this was all of them.

And then there was me…we have already established I felt old, but I was also an extremely shy girl, in fact, most of the time I wanted to be invisible. I never felt like I fitted in at all. All I wanted to do really was just be with my energy friend, who was always with me anyway, but I was just as happy it being the two of us. I was feeling disconnected from this world whilst feeling so connected to another, with no explanation why. I never heard anyone else ever talk about such a feeling. Were there any others out there feeling like me? I felt lost, alone, with half of my body feeling as if it was walking in spirit life with the rest of me in human form. That's exactly what it felt like and how was I to explain such a thing. I was far too young, really, to know how to verbalize my feelings in any depth except to describe it as feeling like an old person/soul in a child's body with the knowing of another world, and the wisdom of many lives.

I tried to figure out reasons in my head why I felt disconnected from this world so much, and after noticing one day that I couldn't see any baby pictures of me around the house, I started to think maybe I was adopted. Could this explain why I felt different? Not that this really made sense to me because I felt very connected to my family that I loved with every part of me. The detachment I felt was from this world, not my family. However, I was trying to piece the puzzle together, so I continually asked my mother for years if I was adopted. I'm sure she took offense at me asking not once but many times, after she had clearly said, "No," because one day she pulled out the hospital baby photos to prove to me I was in fact 'hers'. After that, I never mentioned it again! I know this all sounds quite strange, but I was living in a world that was so foreign to me, and I guess curious to find answers.

So that was all of us making up 'our family'. We were not a materialistic family or about money, greed, or jealousy in any way. We were a normal loving family (with pets!!!) that lived as easy-going and stress-free as possible. My parents kept everything pretty simple; we didn't do drama or get involved with other people's drama. Life was easier that way.

All in all, I felt blessed for my beautiful family who as 'strange as I felt I was' either didn't notice or just let me be.

They never told me I was silly or asked me to give up my invisible friend; it was a loving understanding environment. But I noticed all of this never stopped the feeling that I was missing something inside, as well as the strong feeling that I had been here and done all of this before! Not just once, but hundreds of times!! This was leading me to start asking

"What am I doing here?" And, "Why am I doing this again?"

To this day, as I look back on this little girl and recall those days as I write this. I still struggle to find the words to deliver such an accurate feeling that I've traveled with my whole life. What I have explained here, I feel is as close as I'll ever get, but words escape me still, because there simply are no words.

***

The time had come for me to attend school which was in close proximity to my house, but as it wasn't close enough to walk Mum drove us each day. I wasn't sure about school. I had skipped pre-school the year before because everyone said I was too advanced and didn't need to go. This was a lovely thought, and yes, I was quite advanced, but it seemed kind of strange I didn't go. I was glad I didn't, as that gave me much more time with my energy friend, it gave us another year home together before I had to start sharing him with many others and their possible reactions. (I already knew how that worked, other's reactions, as I had already experienced that one) But starting school would be an interesting experience with how I didn't fit in.

So here I was on my first day of school – a little blondie heading off with her skippy school bag over her shoulder. My bag was quite small, not all that large to fit books, but mind you how many books does a first grader need in all honesty. I wore a pretty summer dress with white socks and black sandals, as our schools in those days didn't have uniforms they were not required.

For those non-Australians, Skippy is, in fact, a Kangaroo, a very famous one that is – he had his own TV show, and it was called Skippy! (Of course). He was kind of an icon in Australia for overseas visitors, but somehow created the impression to the world that we all had a *pet* kangaroo in our backyards that came everywhere with us, this wasn't exactly the truth. If you lived in the country, you regularly saw them and may have even had them in your backyard, but they didn't skip down the streets of Melbourne... Nor any other city for that matter. School was all a bit surreal for me given the way I felt, and because I was extremely shy I kept to myself. I rarely talked (unless it was with my energy friend). I did do my best to make friends under the circumstances, but I was more a loner. I made one good friend and decided I may just stick with them. I didn't hide my energy friend; I didn't talk so much openly like I did at home, but I never hid the fact that I had them with me. Even with having them beside me, though, I have to say I didn't enjoy the experience of being at school much at all. I felt like everyone was too young, and I didn't enjoy being treated like a child. Especially, I suppose, because I felt like I knew more or had been here before, but overall it all felt very odd to me.

I was now at the tender young age of five and unbeknown to me, I was about to experience my first real trauma when our Sailor was hit on the road before my eyes. In all his excitement to greet us returning home from a family holiday, he ran out onto the path of a speeding vehicle and was killed instantly. I raced over to where he was and knelt down beside him to see if he was still breathing, I couldn't see him breathing, but I was assured he was still alive – he had to be. As he lay on the side of the road, my heart was aching. All I could do was lie with him sobbing tears whilst begging him to wake up. He had a red bull ant crawling on him, and I was worried he would be stung and hurt all the time not believing he had already gone. As tears poured down my face, I remember yelling at him to "Wake up, wake up and move, so I can get this bull ant off you", I was yelling at him to wake up. By this stage, I was beside myself and my parents and brother were trying to pull me away, but I wouldn't move. I was five years old and not ready to say goodbye to our beloved dog that greeted me into the family when I was born. He had been around longer than me. I couldn't leave him. My parents were so distressed at how quick it all played out, one minute he was here jumping around us so happy and the next minute he was gone. As they finally pulled me away gently from his side, hugging me they explained he had gone up to heaven and was in a better place. I was so distraught; I didn't want to believe them, but in some way I knew they were telling me the truth, and although so much was still so blurry to me in this life, when they said those words "He's gone up to heaven and was in a better place", I knew they had got that right! Sailors' passing was my first-ever feeling of trauma and loss in this world, and it hit my heart so hard. I became angry at the way it happened, and I saw just how unfair life can be. The driver was swerving as well as speeding when they came around the corner and because of their actions our pet had been killed. People make dumb inconsiderate decisions in life that can effect and hurt others. Not only our beloved Sailor, but because of her bad selfish choices our family were now suffering. People may say he's just a dog, but he was never 'just a dog' to us.

Sailor was not just a family pet; he was always part of our family, protecting my brother and me wherever we went, having fun with us along the way. When the Mr. Whippy ice cream truck played its music from miles away, Sailor would hear it before us, running in and barking to notify us it was 'Ice cream time' because, of course, he got one too. He had rescued my brother one day when he was lost in the paddocks, he ran back home barking to Mum bringing attention as if to say "Come with me I've found him." Sailor led whilst Mum followed and sure enough there was my brother in the bushland. He had pretty much saved my brother's life. He was an amazing dog, and we shared many beautiful moments with him, a normal dog he was not. He was like a human, and although I only shared him for a short time, those memories I still carry. RIP Sailor.

***

Feeling older for my age meant I never really enjoyed interacting with children, but yet listening and conversing with adults, I could do all day. From an early age, I preferred to be around the adults, but the adults couldn't understand why, so I was constantly told to go outside to play with the other children. This was sometimes followed up by 'children should be seen and not heard'. Telling a child, they should be seen and not heard is one of the most harmful things anyone could say to a child. The impact those words have at such a young age is incredibly damaging. Not only does this child feel rejected, worthless feelings are not far behind. I can't even begin to explain how destructive this quote is on so many levels, and each time this was said to me, I felt myself fade away even further to invisibility. Not only did I feel all of the above, but a nuisance as well. My parents never utilized that term once with me; strange how it was always other people who felt they had the privilege.

Children have a voice, and in some cases if they are old souls it's a wise voice. Either way a child should be given the time and heard. These ancient aged-based discriminative myths and sayings that have been handed down through generations upon generations need to be seen for what they are and have been. Outdated actions originated centuries ago by ones in control. If you want a child to leave the room whilst conducting adult conversations there is a better way to ask. In those moments of rejection, I found relief with my energy friend as a soft, gentle, loving feeling – a pure essence that would enter my body overcoming me with a sense of incredible protection and love. I felt extremely grateful that, not only in those moments but every moment, I could always count on my invisible friend.

I was a loner. Even when I wasn't alone, I felt alone. I never ever lost the feeling that there was another home we belonged to in some other place. Have you ever just known you reside someplace else, intuitively feeling? Or not being able to shake the feeling there's someone else you are a part of? Well I did, and I can tell you it's one persistent feeling that never goes away – not that I wanted it to, because it was part of me. However, that feeling lingered from a very early age and along with my timid nature, covered up by a nervous personality. I struggled. It's not easy to try and fit in when you don't. I didn't want people to see the real me. I was like a little lost soul in a human body, being introverted coupled with extreme shyness. Thank goodness, I had my 'shadow' walking with me. I felt them walking and guiding me all the time.

There was no secret, I did not hide my invisible friend from anyone, but the time came when others didn't appreciate me being so open about it. To me, it felt so normal, and I didn't care if it was frowned upon. However, it appeared society had a different view. Behaviors of this kind are all cute, innocent, and laughable to a certain age. But once a child starts to become older, it's no longer acceptable in the ways of this world. I had been at school a couple of years now, and as 'weird' as I may have seemed to others my energy friend came first. I didn't seem to care at school what they thought, as I kept to myself a lot. Even being around my few friends was okay, as I still explained about my energy friend to them, and they didn't judge me at all, they believed me. We would still talk away to each other having conversations at school, even if someone did hear me 'which looked like I was talking to myself', my loyalty to us was extraordinary, because this was us and we walked together and in my mind there was no doubt of ever disobeying that. Why would I ever want to? I accepted others for who they were, I didn't think they were strange for not being old souls or having an energy friend with them, so why couldn't people extend me the same courtesy. I was starting to figure out though it doesn't work that way in this world.

I could never have imagined letting go of my invisible energy friend as they were part of me, and I knew I wouldn't have survived, but at around seven years of age something happened that forced this situation upon me. I no longer felt I could publicly keep acknowledging my friend like it was natural to me. This feeling was brought upon me with a particular incident that I recall quite clearly. We were having one of our Friday fun nights where friends and extended family would come over and either play cards, dance, or just sit around having a drink and catch up. Of course, my energy friend was with me, as always, and as always this was not usually a problem. Everyone knew about my friend, and although I had succumbed to the giggles and raised eyebrows over time, I still felt free to express the little girl inside and her friend. After all, it felt we were joined together so why wouldn't I acknowledge them. This specific night started out feeling like any other Friday night, I was just being myself like always but after referring to my invisible friend someone decided that it was *not* okay to do that anymore. They spoke up to give their opinion followed by another then another, and the tone of their voices this time was different to others, to me it was heartless and brutal.

"Come on, that's enough. This is ridiculous, how long are you going to keep going on with this nonsense, talking to your 'invisible friend' when there is no one there."

I was speechless: one by one other's followed saying much the same whilst laughing at me, as I stood there listening. I started to feel numb. My parents had said nothing to this point but one of our guests looked towards them and said:

"It's time she grew out of this now; this has been going on long enough, and it's time you did something about it. Maybe you need to take her to see someone, a doctor perhaps, because people will think she's crazy, or they will start thinking something is wrong with her, and you will be responsible if anything happens. This type of thing is okay when they're young, but she's old enough now to have grown out of it. You can't just keep letting it go."

Some of the other's followed on saying similar things, and as these words were spoken in front of me, I felt something happen. Their words became blurred underneath the noise of their laughter, they were all laughing not just about me, but at me. It came totally unexpected, and I was mortified. My parents had never spoken or treated me this way before, and never would. They had always let me be, and to them if I still wanted to have my friend they didn't care. If it made me happy, they were happy. But others didn't quite see it this way, and they chose to express their thoughts to my parents, in front of me, an innocent little girl, whilst they knew I could hear every word they said. As I looked at my parents for their reaction, I don't think they knew what to say. I didn't understand why I may be taken to see a doctor or why people thought I might be crazy; I didn't understand. But I understood the pain, the crushing humiliation and embarrassment. Everyone was laughing at me. They made me feel I was doing something very wrong, and why was it wrong, why was expressing who I was and what I could feel, see, and connect to so wrong. I had talked about and shown my friend publicly since I was old enough to verbalize, and I never felt I had to change anything or change me. But there was something about these words this time, they were different.

My little heart broke. It was my first taste of direct harsh judgment, and I felt ashamed. I felt they were insinuating I was stupid and that no one would ever understand the real me. I also felt this overwhelming emotion to protect what was mine, protect us, where no person could ever come between us or split us apart. Where no one would ever talk so disrespectful of my energy friend, or dishonor the love they brought or how amazing they were to me again. I didn't know how to say 'dishonor' at seven years of age but that's exactly what it felt like. They had dishonored us. I was angry inside that these people could treat my 'spirit' friend like they never existed, and perhaps, angry at myself for feeling so out of my depth that I didn't stand up for us. I was also scared that they may take me to a doctor because I didn't understand what all that was about. Many things went through my head that night and fear became my driver. There was a lot I may not have understood yet in this weird world of ours and given my age, but one thing I understood was the way I felt and how they made me feel. I was completely devastated, and I wondered how they could do this to a little girl. *I wondered, was this my welcome to this world*.

As I went to bed that night feeling sad and broken, I was thinking what I would do. My friend was still with me, I could feel them, but I had realized that night I was way too sensitive for this world. What happened was enough for me to see that if it was this hard to fit in, how was I ever going to fit in with others if I didn't conform to what is acceptable. I would be constantly laughed at, and they would never understand me. Why does it have to be this way? Why can we not accept that some enter this world with 'eyes wide open' about where they have come from, along with a remembrance of the spirit world? Why are we so primitive in this world to not understand or 'Remember'?

From that day on, my energy friend started to fade, and so did my light.

Chapter 3
The Change... Time to Mask

For a seven-year-old, I did comprehend much more than a normal child my age, I guess it was that old/advanced soul coming out in me, but most saw me as a little adult. My family even saw I was way beyond my years and treated me as such. How does one know they are advanced as a soul? To be honest, I can only explain from my own experience, and it was just a knowing, a knowing of how to do things, what to say, a knowing of feeling a lot older than people around me, in some cases even adults, as I felt I had a deeper understanding about life than they did, it's a desire to be alone or a loner, a feeling like you've been here and done it all before. All these are signs of being an advanced soul. For me, it was just something inside, along with the pull to the other world, whereof, I remembered a great deal. Plus, of course, I had my energy friend that showed me many things. By that I mean intuitively guiding me day to day, helping me to navigate the easiest path. Which I listened to wholeheartedly, because I still thought this is how it should be. I also sought out elderly people to talk to because I felt I had something in common with them, plus I enjoyed our conversations. Sometimes they just saw me as a kid, which didn't really help, but most saw that I was advanced for my age. Our elderly neighbor across the road became my friend, and I would visit her frequently to chat, listening to her about life and experiences. I don't know that anyone can fully explain or give descriptive insight to how you know you're an old soul. You just know.

That being said, as I woke the next morning, from my ordeal the night before, I realized a change had to be made. The more I had engaged with others showing my true self the more I was thought to be strange. When I exerted my wisdom and knowledge of things with those who were older, I was often put down and quickly put in my place as a silly kid. I just wanted to be me and be accepted for who I was. But it didn't seem to be working out too well from my outward experience. I wanted to be happy and live from this beautiful peacefulness I felt within. I wanted things simple. However, I couldn't feel this beautiful euphoric love here on earth that I knew existed, which confused me. Why wasn't it here? And why were others not living from this love?

As much as I could understand so much more, I couldn't comprehend why people were not accepting me or my energy friend. Why did they find us so odd? I guess because it wasn't the way of the world, the physical world we reside in. But this love and higher consciousness was available to everyone, not just me, so why didn't they? Why were they not tapping into their own higher consciousness to help navigate *their* way, why were they not *remembering* like I was? Maybe they all didn't have an attached energy in spirit like me, but they all had the resources to connect to their hearts to their soul and live from love and kindness. They didn't seem to know of the love and light that I knew of and this appeared bizarre to me. I had to think of what to do being different in a world like ours, so without feeling I had a choice, I realized if I was going to fit in as 'normal' in any kind of way, I would have to change. (Not that I saw them all as normal, it felt quite abnormal to me to be honest). But hence, I slowly started to change, conform, to make it easier for myself in that moment, and disguise my true self by layering with a mask.

I later met in my adult life people like me who had known their entire life of this universal light and love. They had continued sharing it with others, despite being thought crazy. They remained open and awake; they didn't care what others thought. I admired their courage and self-love to remain their true selves in this crazy world of the matrix; however, I was way too sensitive to criticism and didn't have that fearlessness.

So on went the first mask, and I took on the patterns of what children are 'supposed' to do and say and closed up even

27

further. All that I used to see – angel wings, energy, spirits – were no longer visible to me. The feeling that I was living between two worlds started to close up, and I sunk deeper inside myself becoming further introverted. It was kind of like letting go of everything I knew to be right, true, authentic and stepping into a world that was false, controlled, and strange. Things just never added up. But yet when I looked around at these people living here, they seemed to not understand; they lived like this was it, all there was. I had no idea why they didn't get it, or couldn't feel what I did.

Surprisingly, the only thing that didn't go away or shut down was feeling my energy friend. I may not have been able to see any more, but for some reason I could feel the energy could still get through. Why was it still able to connect with me when I'd lost so much of my connection with the other world? I was feeling more connected now within this world and less in the other. I didn't feel as light, happy, innocent, and free anymore. It felt considerably heavier in this world than the other, which made sense given what I'd just experienced. When I noticed the energy was still present, I realized for the first time just how connected we were, how deeply rooted, within our soul. This energy was not leaving me; it seemed I could not disconnect from it no matter how much I had disconnected from my true self. It may have faded which I first thought, but then I realized its power had returned fully when I did not hide it. My light dulled to the outside world because of my masks, but inside, in my own internal world, I could still feel the depth of this love with such power. Wow, if this is what people called your guardian angel, it certainly was powerful. Although mine felt a lot different to how others talk about it. The protection from this energy was extraordinary; it had my back in every way.

As the days moved on, it was still walking with me but not talking as much, or was it still talking to me the same? Maybe it still was, but I couldn't hear as much anymore. I had **shut myself down** in many ways to not be ridiculed, laughed at, but yet I could still feel the energy there. They were quieter, but I could hear them when they chose to speak, telepathy was the way I heard them but just not as often. My friend never talked out loud so others could hear them, of course that's not how spirits work, you just hear them talk to you and see or feel their presence. I had now created a situation where I had to act like someone completely different whilst still feeling this energy with me, and it was harder than I thought. I was torn in two, torn between – do I hide them, or do I keep sharing so I can feel more myself, more us. The decision felt excruciating for me; I was always loyal to us no matter how much I got thrown at me in my life so far, but this was difficult. I started to feel traumatized at the thought of losing my friend, losing that part of me, because that was me, but I didn't know if I had it in me to suffer the humiliation from others. Do I act like this experience is not happening to me and just hide it away within myself and from others, only connecting and talking to my friend when I'm alone. Perhaps, this was the better way, but this saddened me. I felt alone even though I knew they were there, and I knew whatever I chose they would help me to get through. So did this mean I didn't trust myself? It felt like I had already decided but what was I doing? What experience had I now created?

"For what is not viewed by the naked eye, does not mean it is not present."

It's bizarre, isn't it, how easily we listen to others and do what they say, worrying about what they think of us. Telling ourselves, because they are adults, they know best. Immediately our ego, mind is activated, and we believe there is something wrong with us. At such an early age, this can be brutal to some children and rather than to stay connected to our soul, we drift into a false reality driven by ego. I wished back then I had more of an understanding of what was going on with me, so I could have avoided the ego paradigm that most were living in. I may not have realized it at this point, but it was at that crucial time for me when children transition from being spiritually open to spiritually closed, what we usually refer to as 'staying awake in that higher consciousness from birth' to falling asleep into the society paradigm. It's difficult for a child to remain in that enlightened state when catapulted into such extreme society programming. Most find that when they hit school age, they forget what they once may have been able to see or feel, such as spirits, energy and angels. Those beings/souls have not really disappeared. The innocence of the child has started to slip away, feelings get hurt, emotions take over, and the ego is born! This is how a child falls into the lower dimensional energies of our reality, and thus becomes 'asleep'.

I didn't really forget, or accidently fall 'asleep', despite my feelings being hurt, and my ego acting out accordingly. I was still very much awake, trying to make myself 'forget' and fall asleep. How messed up is that! All just so I could fit in with others and not be called weird or bullied, all so I wasn't labeled as different.

However, the question I should have been asking myself through all of this was,

"Why did I want to be the same?"

Being your true self, despite how weird or different you may feel, is better than layering masks to fit in and being someone you're not.
Us weird different people are here for a reason. Us weird different people are here to shine our light!!!
Not hide it!!!

There's something about school that catapults everything to a different level for young children, and I wasn't any different. It was becoming increasingly hard for me to cover up my energy friend (not that really I wanted to) along with how different I saw life compared to others, so I needed a survival tool. For how long I needed this to get me through life I wouldn't know, but until I was more confident and had the courage to reveal myself again this was my only choice. This way people would not know the real me; I needed a mask (one of many that I would develop over time) to create my false self. Being painfully shy and introverted didn't help when it came to figuring out how I would do this. I didn't know where to start.

We tend to learn how to layer with masks (our true authentic selves) when we don't want to be seen, visible for judgment. We keep that sacred part of us so hidden inside to escape potential heartbreak. I was no different; I had been crushed by people's jokes and reactions, judgment, and criticism. Being sensitive meant, I never stood up for myself to say.

"Hey listen, this is real, and I'd much rather be having my experience than yours. You all look like you are in pain," but how does a child, old soul or not, say that to others.

Strange as it may seem given my nature, the mask I chose was to talk. Yes I know, very odd, but I saw it like this. Talking took the focus off me and projected it upon others because I could choose the topic. I communicated now as a talker, a nervous one, but it helped not to expose who I really was as a soul. I was able to create a whole new personality from covering up by talking, people saw a different me, not the real one. That way anything so sacred to me deep inside was untouchable, no one could take from me what was mine, no one could mess with my heart, soul, nor my energy friend. I locked it away from the world all so nice and tight, but not realizing by doing so I disconnected from my true self... And my soul.

***

For me, my favorite place was home with my family. Having an older brother worked well for me the way I felt, so often I would be found playing in bush cubby houses, playing football, tippity run cricket (which it was called in my state) or playing with train and Scalextric racing car sets. These really did excite me, much more than playing with dolls. Along with these, I listened to music as music was my ultimate love, and this was how I spent most of my spare time. I never was one for dolls – much to my mum's disappointment, but she was happy I was passionate about dancing, as she had been a dancer herself. Dancing connected me with my soul and allowed me to open my heart to feeling free.

Because of this, I danced every day; music fed my soul from an early age and dancing was a form of expressing my true self.

Music in my home was diverse – my mother was a huge Elvis Presley fan, so we often had his songs blasting out through the house, which I didn't mind because they were fun upbeat tracks. My brother's passion was always music, and he spent many hours over the record player, taping, editing, and remixing music from a very young age. As I've mentioned, he was music crazy, *which is probably where I got it from,* so neither of us would possibly survive without it. When Elvis didn't have the floor, my brother would be listening to his vinyls, the likes of The Sweet, The Angels, Fleetwood Mac, Blondie, Pink Floyd, Cheap Trick, ABBA, Elton John to a stack of disco one hit wonders of the '70s and more! The list was so diverse you never knew what would be blaring out from the player, which made it so much fun.

He had been collecting the latest '45s since he was five years old, each week my parents buying him another, so music was very much a constant in our home. It also enabled me to be acquainted with artists I wouldn't have yet known or be listening to given our age difference. The music influence around me was how I developed an appreciation for several genres, not just the ones of 'my' era. I loved blues, classical, jazz, Rock and Roll as well as the '70s music influence that my brother listened to.

He also loved to dance like me, and so our passion for dance had us creating and choreographing dance routines on a regular basis. We loved doing this together each day, and it soon became part of us. Creating movement from our free spirit was exciting for us, we loved it. We were both fairly talented at dance but never really took it beyond our living room.

My parents were hard workers and had saved enough to build my mum's dream home as she called it. She designed the home herself, and to my surprise (as I never really took much notice before it was built) I couldn't believe this beautiful home we had now moved into. I was aware how fortunate I was. We were not a wealthy family by any means, just hard workers which had produced and provided a lovely family home for us all. It was a double story and consisted of three extremely large bedrooms plus one average size study. We had two living areas, one on the ground floor and one upstairs, balconies lined the front and rear of the home, and the land extended to the street behind. It sounds large but Dad needed somewhere to park his truck, so a smaller property wouldn't have sufficed. (Those trucks are monsters). Mum selected the décor which was the 'way out' colors of the '70s, but no one really worried about matching anything back then. I was most grateful she never went for the huge swirls and abstract designs; instead, it was all quite plain. I felt blessed to have this comfortable home to call mine, as I had awareness that not all children in the world could say the same. I was fortunate to live in a country where this was feasible, where my parents could work hard and be able to afford to build us a beautiful home with a loving family environment.

The Peninsula was part of the coast 90 minutes south from the bright lights and big city of Melbourne. It was a picturesque scenic destination which sat between bay and ocean waters. The bay beach was now at my doorstep, the ocean beach was a ten-minute drive away. The Peninsula was a mixture with beaches, upbeat trendy coastal shops in the exclusive parts of town, to farming areas that felt like you were living in the country. You could travel up to the Hills, apple orchards, vineyards, strawberry, and cherry farms. Go on cliff walks to lighthouses and collect your fresh fruit and veggies from the local markets or farms. It was a healthy lifestyle and relaxing way to live (If you took notice). We could travel ten minutes in each direction and find ourselves amongst such diverse surroundings. When you thought about it, although small, it was an extremely beautiful place to live if you didn't want the buzz city lifestyle.

As our Saturday mornings rolled around, it was always exciting getting up early and running downstairs to switch on the TV. Why? Because Saturday mornings was *Cartoon Morning* … (Who *'didn't'* watch cartoons on Saturday's?)

I was up bright and early for the ones that would start at 6 am. Why so early you might ask? Well, because although I wasn't even a thought in my parents mind when *The Thunderbirds* were created. I was a fan, and they always seemed to be on at some ridiculous hour of the morning. I probably didn't even understand them so much, it was more my brother's choice. I was a *Jetsons* girl in all honesty, but something about *The Thunderbirds* just lured me in. My other favorites, I never missed on a Saturday morning, were *The Flintstones* because if you hadn't heard Fred scream out 'Wilma' or 'Yabba Dabba Doo', then your morning wasn't complete. Others I enjoyed with anticipation were *Scooby-Doo*, *Archie*, *Josie and the Pussycats*, *Wonder Woman*, *Superman* and let's not forget *HR Pufnstuff.* (Who's your friend when things get rough?) Indeed!

Of course, back then in my era they were all repeats. And if you didn't belong to this era you are probably thinking to yourself "What is she going on about". As I look back on them now, they probably do look a little lame to younger generations. But remember, this was a time of a great deal more innocence, where fun, light, and fluffy T.V shows and cartoons were on the agenda, not so much the violent and darker ones of today.

My dad surprised us one day with buying the new color television that had been released in Australia. They had already long been released in the United States and other countries, but Australia was always a little behind getting the latest technology appliances. I was very happy because from then on my cartoons and T.V shows became a whole lot more interesting not to mention fun to watch. All these activities, and more, I enjoyed whilst being in the presence of my beautiful energy friend. Home was where I felt so comfortable, and I let my guard down. Home was where the little lost shy girl was not so lost.

Through these times, my parents became best friends with another couple, and we shared much time together with the result of our families becoming extremely close. They had five children of varying ages which my brother and I hung out with some weekends. Those children were perhaps the only others that got a glimpse into who I was – my shy, weird, naïveté with this world – but although I was more open around them, I had still kept my energy friend a secret. They knew of my imaginary friend earlier but now, like others, they thought it was long gone. I had never expressed to the extent of how I felt this energy or explained in length the details to anyone. My mother's best friend (their mum) was like an aunt to me; actually, she was more like a second mum. She made me feel comfortable to be around which was a godsend for me, and her family was easy going and down to earth, straight to the point authentic people, which I loved. We had great times involving lots of fun together over the years. I have beautiful fond memories of her, the family, and our time together.

**

My father and I were very close. He worked a lot but weekends, when he was off work, were weekends I loved even more. Dad was an exceptionally quiet man; he thought a lot, but said very little, unless it needed to be said. In some way, without us ever talking about me or 'who I was' I think he figured me out, or at least figured I felt different. He seemed to get the deeper side of me. The fact he never judged or criticized or tried to change me established this trust between us. As a man or father, he could have felt embarrassed by me being shy and different, but he never was. He always showed me nothing but unconditional love.

Hence, I was Dad's girl and spending time with him was so special to me. On weekends, I would be wherever he was, which was often working underneath his 22-wheeler semi-truck. I can't say I was much help, but I learnt a lot. I did love using the grease gun and getting my hands dirty, not sure why because in other ways I hated getting dirty. But I was so happy and thankful that dad took the time to teach me. I would also end up in various other places helping him when he wasn't working on the truck. I may have been helping him in his shed, or his bird Aviary. Again, it wasn't about getting my hands dirty, but rather about spending time with him and the things he liked to do. To a little girl, his truck was a huge rig (well it was) and I remember my favorite part was climbing up into the cabin eager to pull on that chain.

"Can I, Dad, please?"

"No, Kell."

"Ohh, please, Dad?"

"No, Kellie, you will scare my birds!"

"Well, it's just this once, pleaseeee," (although it never was just once).

"Well just a quick one then and only 'ONCE' (rolling his eyes, because he knew it wasn't just once. He knew next weekend I'd be asking again).

"Thanks, Dad," (I'd say with a huge smile on my face).

Within seconds, I would reach for that chain (most times my hand was already there) pulling it down to hear that deep loud truckie's air horn echo throughout the neighborhood. I loved the sound of a revving engine and the horn on a truckies rig. In Australia, we call them truckies, other countries I think they were known as truckers. (Something I picked up from the 'gazillion' times I watched the movie 'Convoy'). Sitting up in that cabin with my father felt amazing, even seeing them glide along the open road like they owned it gave me goose bumps. Those days I cherish. I was not a tom boy, and I didn't particularly like dirt and grease, but there was just something about trucks that excited me.

Sharing these days with my father was very special to me. He was an avid bird breeder and very passionate about his hobby, along with golfing and fishing. He taught me to play golf as early as I could hold up a club and swing, I'm not sure how far the ball went, but he was always encouraging. I loved golf because of the peacefulness. It was around nature where everyone had to be quiet; no one really talked. He played competition golf each Saturday morning and often brought home a trophy, as he was quite the impressive golfer – of course, and I was so proud of him.

Fishing was also another sport or hobby he loved, so fishing we shared… And just like the golfing, we would go fishing. Venturing out in our 18-foot-boat to catch flathead on the bay most weekends (weather permitting) was so relaxing on the water. Such peace and serenity was magic to me. We often went as a family and Mum would pack all the essentials for the day. Sandwiches, hotdogs, fruit, and buns, she had it all worked out with her flasks of 'everything for every occasion' We never went hungry and by the end of the day we had always caught plenty of fish for dinner. I was probably a little better at fishing than golfing to be honest, since dropping a line over the side of the boat was a fair bit easier than putting that little white ball into a tiny hole. This was my survival for me. Spending time around my family, being home, where I could be more myself.

However, when I had to be around others, I usually gravitated to children I could see were as lost as me. I was good at spotting those ones. I figured we could be lost together.

Living here, I could see, was turning out to be a difficult task being an advanced soul, but at the same time it should have been a privilege. It was a privilege, if only I could stay out of my ego mind. However, we are all given 'free will' which means despite what we came here for, what purpose in life we have chosen to fulfil; our free-will ego can often get in the way sending us off path. It can then become difficult for us to live our best lives. To fulfil what we have chosen, how to serve ourselves and others. This can only be shown through our true authentic selves and our higher intuition. I didn't know this at the time, but the universe will always push you back on track, and unless you stop resisting, it will keep pushing for however long it takes.

Imagine traveling with the purest form of love that ignites your whole inner being. An unexplainable form of light/energy integrating with your body, your soul, your own energy. Envisage the highest level of purification, protection, and unconditional love – a love that makes you want to disappear with them into their world. This is what it felt like; this incredible love is what I was blessed with. When I sat, it was like having someone sit beside me. When I walked, I never walked alone. When I was in my room, it was a stronger presence than ever. It was with me everywhere and as I got older I wondered, what or who was I really feeling and talking to? My heart would say, if I talked and acknowledged it enough, perhaps, I may just manifest it into my reality. I wanted my friend to be in human form with me, nothing felt more right than this. I couldn't really understand why they weren't. I knew if they were here, my absent feeling would be no longer. However, as much as I felt my soul was calling to them to come and join me, it remained an energy form.

Chapter 4
Greater Love

By now, the War in Vietnam was over and celebrations had echoed around the globe. There's something about war that leaves an impact on many and Vietnam was no exception. At such an early age, I could see this world was not perhaps a pleasant place to be. However, if we could bring peace and love to the world, then maybe no one ever had to experience war again. I wanted to help bring peace and love to the world. Why wasn't everyone trying harder to do this, to join as one? Why was there racism, famine, hatred, and war? It never made sense to me. We had world renowned singers like John Lennon, Bob Dylan, Cat Stevens, Bob Marley, The Beetles, and many more singing their songs about a world where everyone shares love, compassion, and kindness. They were helping spread the message and educate the greater masses, but who was really listening, because from what I saw growing up, most of the world lived in judgment and fear. I wasn't aware back then just how the system worked, but whilst there was always going to be a selected group of people running the world the way they did. Would it ever be any different?

It was the '70s, and if I wanted to fit in instead of feeling like an outcast, I had to 'Get with it' as they say. Having an older brother was an advantage for learning the appropriate slang words; because it all felt quite alien to me.

So here we go: People were cool or cool cats, if it was super cool it was 'off the hook' and if it was exceptionally cool it was 'outta sight' (there were levels to this 'cool' thing, and you needed to know your slang). Things were 'groovy' (especially if you listened to Marcia Brady). Some got 'psyched out', while others were catching each other on the 'flip side.' If there was no chance of something happening, it was 'dream on' and the most common one I'm pretty sure was 'far out'. 'You're a total spaz' was quite derogatory but very popular. Something that was 'Bangin' meant it was good, if you got 'busted' it meant you were doing something you shouldn't be doing. To 'dig it' meant do you understand, 'chill' was to stay cool, 'boogie' was dancing and 'do you copy' was well used on the CB radio. 'Funky' could cut both ways being cool or weird. There were many more, far too many to mention, in fact you could probably write a book on '70s slang. But here, I've chosen the more common or innocent ones. For an era that now sounds 'daggy' (yes, that's another one), it was actually a pretty 'happening' decade. (Oh and another)

I actually think the '70s slang had a lot of fun to it, and some of these sayings were commonly used through other decades.

As we were the first generation to experience both parents working and having to become more independent, it was time for me to start walking to school since school was in close proximity (the end of my street to be precise). Being home alone after school was new for me though; it was becoming the new way of the world.

By now, several years had passed by during which I had kept my friend a secret. Those who knew of me having an invisible friend when I was younger simply thought it had disappeared, or I had grown out of it back then. They never realized it was still with me or that I always felt it. Of course, it was different from my younger days when I had the place set at the dining table, we were long past that, since it was all hidden. In addition, in those days, I could obviously see more, but these days, as I got older, it was just there. It faded at times depending on my level of connection with myself. Becoming older was increasingly interesting to say the least on how I felt the energy drift in and out, which was 'all my doing'! It still wasn't the type of thing you shared even if I did rename my invisible friend as an energy presence. That sounded more mature, and perhaps, even possible to some. However, in these times not many talked about spirituality or metaphysics.

The missing piece had become a constant within me, like a deep empty void I couldn't fill. I started living less from my true self and more from someone else. As the energy presence surged in (when I opened to it), that feeling of something missing felt less present; however, there was still a degree of missing or yearning for something I couldn't grasp, most likely because I was in the physical world. In every part of my soul, my being, I knew it should be here with me as well. Why? Because every part of me felt it joined my soul in completion so why wouldn't it be here with me, why would we be physically separated, it didn't make sense, but at the same time I felt we were quite unique.

Many times I tried to reach out and pull it into reality with me, as extreme as that sounds. But, honestly, who wouldn't try? Who wouldn't want this beautiful energy with them in physical form? A part of me felt I could, until I realized that I couldn't. (Because it wasn't happening) I wanted to see what it was or who it was. It was all a mystery. What purpose did it have in my life, with me? Obviously, this particular being was connected to me, but did others have ones connected to them too, and were they sharing the same experience? If not, why not? I had so many questions and no answers. Yet despite the fact it sounds confusing it wasn't, because there was this absolute sense of knowing it was right. That it was meant to be. In my heart and soul, I knew this connection was forever real, authentic, more than any physical experience I was having, and I was extremely fortunate to have it.

So as my days grew longer, and the nights more lonely (having zero luck bringing this energy into *my* world), I filled my time with hobbies and fun activities with my brother and our close friends. I was still dancing every day because dancing was where I could always feel him, *(*yes him, it was more of a masculine energy feeling I sensed now*)* and also where I could feel myself. Where I could feel that extraordinary infinite love. I realized then, in those moments, that I had always known true love exists, and it exists with me somehow.

***

Love

Let me share a deeper understanding about love, because after all this chapter is about 'Greater Love'.

We look at love many different ways, which makes sense because there are many different kinds of love. Some have had greater love experiences than others, and therefore can attest to these incredible powerful kinds of love beyond all else. Some are yet to experience these incredible loves, and believe it or not there are some people that don't believe in 'Soulmates' or 'the one' at all. Maybe these people have had an experience of searching their whole life to have yet found their 'one', and so this has led them to believe that soulmates don't exist. Perhaps, that's okay, because maybe not everyone is here to feel a deeper love in this lifetime. They may be here this time for a different experience.

Some may have encountered a traumatic experience with love leaving them broken hearted, forcing them to have shut down their heart. When we shut down our heart, it usually results in being unable to find our soulmate. Because if you are not opening your heart, it's rare you will attract them into your life. A closed heart will not attract a deeper love.

There are different types of 'love' on earth. Why? Because, as humans, we have created conditional love – love attached with conditions. Very few of us live from 'Unconditional love'. So the experience we outwardly create for ourselves will be one of conditioned love.

The love I felt my entire life was unconditional euphoric love with a feeling of complete sacredness. So I knew this love existed, the love that people dream of. I had no idea how or when I would ever find this true love, but I knew it was out there and in some way it would find me!

I used to dream, and in those dreams I was shown and told that this love would come to me. In whatever form that was, I had no idea but it would come. I always believed in love, not just the 'earthly conditioned' love we were taught, but a complete and utter all-encompassing consuming incredible love. A love so powerful that it feels like time stands still. A love so special and rare. A love that stands as all there is. A love where nothing else matters – where everything in life is second to this love, and creating from this love is magical. Magical beyond all human awareness, interference, and distractions. Because a love like this is infinite, and the power of that love, means that nothing can stand in the way. This was the love I was shown. This was the love I knew to be.

I guess consequently it was much easier for me to know of this love, as it was the love my energy friend brought with him. It was unconditional and pure; a love not experienced often in this world. In fact, I'd only ever heard this love being referenced or spoken about with people that had near death experiences. They had passed over from some kind of accident or health situation only to come back to life in their physical body. Through their experiences, they explain the love relating to nothing like we see or feel on earth. A love that which is weightless, unconditional, pure high energy, no fear based limitations or attachments. After speaking of this extraordinary love and their profound experiences, most usually step onto a more spiritual path.

Well this is what our love felt like, I didn't need to die and go to 'heaven' or have a near death experience to feel it. I felt it in my friend; the energy walking with me through life. And one day the universe would bless me with this love in my physical world. I had no doubt.

Love can also show up in other ways that may be relatable I discovered.

I had an infinity and love for red roses. To me, it was the ultimate symbol of infinite love. From the first time I looked at a red rose, I was drawn to a feeling inside that somehow a red rose meant more to me than just a nice flower that looked pretty. I'm not saying a red rose is not beautiful, it sure is. However, there was more to red roses than I could piece together in this life at this time.

Have you ever felt or been drawn to something that you just can't explain. The connection you have, the knowing of some importance. Knowing that it means so much to you, but yet you have not experienced a situation in your life where that has any significance. Well this situation was just like that. I couldn't explain why, but each red rose was magical to me. It was a representation of pure perfection and sacredness. Decades later, as an adult, I was surprised to finally find out just why 'red roses' held such sacredness deep within my soul, and again I learned to never underestimate YOUR power of intuitive feeling.

***

Albert Einstein once said:

"The more wisdom you attain, and the more conscious you become, the crazier you will appear to others."

Crazy or Gifted – they are one and the same.

This was a quote that always stuck in my mind because I realized it was my fear. If I really showed my wisdom, my intuition to others, I would appear crazy. So this is why 'in the society box I stayed'!

Living in a world full of conditions, paradigms, rules, rights and wrongs, all dictated by society and laws, is not easy on anyone, least of all on a person that doesn't fit in or feels like an old soul. I understood the term 'living in a box', and could see from an early age that most people followed this same pattern. I seemed to feel constantly restrained that I needed to live outside the box. I didn't even want to put one toe in the box, but in a world where everyone around you seems to 'live in the box'; it requires a lot of courage to remain your true self. I'm not sure if it was my shyness or introverted nature that couldn't find that courage, or I felt tired and took the easy way because I didn't understand. However, I have so much admiration for those that rebel to not live 'in the box', or the system, and just BE who they are, their true authentic self, plain, and simple. At this point in my life, I wasn't able to do that.

"We reap what we sow; we experience what we create. If we live creating from fear and resistance, rather than love, that's what we will receive. Our life will rarely flow; we will seldom feel free, and we will never be aligned."

My connection to my 'other' home I still felt, the one I knew to be beyond this physical life – where I had come from.

The one I felt so connected to all through my early years, but it was now significantly weaker. My gifts of seeing, feeling, and being able to interact with that world then had also faded, but when I really sat in my own silence the connection would strengthen. I believed so strongly in angels, and I knew they were around me, but I had no idea how it all worked. I never feared when I was alone that something would happen to me, I always felt safe because I knew I was protected in so many ways.

Something I grew fond of was reading, and I would read in my room alone really absorbing myself into the stories. I went from Dr. Seuss to discovering author Enid Blyton and enjoyed how they could take me above and beyond; her fascinating children's books 'in some way' made me feel a little less weird. Such a talented writer. She wrote on a range of topics, but her fantasy and mystery was what appealed to me the most; she had a way of transporting you into a magical world unlike ours. I was still searching for answers so it was no surprise her books enticed me; they were different to anything I'd read.

The one thing I knew one thousand percent was that I was not imagining anything I was feeling. I had brought it in with me as a reminder of who I was, where I was from, and to keep me on track. A reminder that I was undertaking a journey in life for something special, and I didn't realize till many years later that some other people were having similar experiences to me.

Enid Blyton's books became quite controversial, and it was said she was either using a ghost writer or channeling her many books. This was because she was writing so many per year. She proved she wasn't using a ghost writer so that came back to her obviously channeling them from her higher awareness. Whatever purpose she was meant to serve for humanity, I don't know. However, she was certainly helping children to maintain their innocence and consciousness. This was obviously transcended through her writing, whilst streaming from her higher wisdom. Her books were quite amazing for children, in my opinion, and were a great treasure to explore. I loved reading them and as I finished one, my mum would buy me the next *as a special treat* so I could explore her many topics. Before long my book shelf comprised of many Enid Blyton's.

Reading, being in silence and alone may have been one of my favorite things but so was my passion for music. I listened to tracks every night after school; music was part of my lifeline (to which life I'm not exactly sure). I developed a love for the band 'Kiss', paint masks, rock music, costumes and characters, what can I say? I was drawn to weird and eccentric, as some parts of yourself you just can't cover up.

Australia had the television show *Countdown* hosted by Molly Meldrum from '70s well into the '80s, and it became the most iconic music program in television history. It set the stage for loads of international artists with a random mix of genres. Molly became so well known internationally that just about every international artist that hit our Australian shores would show up on the Countdown stage. You never knew who you would see perform live each week from your living room, and that made it exciting. It truly changed the face of music in our country and each Sunday night, I was glued to the television watching all the new bands and music. It was a good thing we possessed two televisions, because my parents didn't share mine and my brothers same enthusiasm for *Countdown*.

School, however, was another story and to me it became increasingly boring. I didn't fit in with my age group in primary school. Going to class, watching other children, I just knew I had done this all before. I really had no desire to play with others, as I felt I had nothing in common with them. I tried my best but was typically found with one or maybe two friends at most. My spiritual influence I may have hid but everyone could see there was something different about me, that I didn't fit in with others. I suppose you could say I kind of stood out although did my best not to. Sometimes I was laughed at and picked on for it, and although I shouldn't have taken any notice, it was difficult being sensitive. Every word, laugh, or form of embarrassment cut deep into my heart, showing me to hide even more. For me, it was feeding my weakest fear.

Some parts no matter how hard I tried, I just couldn't mask well. I spent lots of time alone in school, as I grew older which became even more obvious, more obvious that I was a loner. The loner…wanting to be alone.

How to fit into a world designed a particular way when you felt so incredibly different. To this day, I can't ever recall a time where I truly felt like I fitted into this world, and probably still don't. Although the difference today is, I have an understanding why and the wisdom to blend the two.

I would have loved someone to teach me back then that being yourself was okay; in fact, it was all you had to be. Say it and live it like it was. No pretending. Reality is, though, not many people on this planet live from their true self – from their heart and soul, because most live from 'Fear not Love'

I grew up in an era where if we thought we were a good person or liked ourselves we were mocked for loving ourselves. The term 'you love yourself' was thrown around so quickly in such a negative manner. Instead of defending ourselves in our honor, we would fight against them saying "No, we don't". Can you believe that now, we actually thought we had to say we didn't love ourselves to conform; we had to show others that loving yourself was bad. Feeling good about who you were was not acceptable and one would never 'love' themselves because that was wrong. The ridiculous complexities of it all.

I was now tall for my age, super slim, long blonde hair, and didn't like that my hips stood out, but every girl seemed to hate something about their body. Although I must say body image wasn't something I bothered about too much till I was older. I searched and searched to find a way to be myself in front of others but my early public display of embarrassment, I think, had scarred me for life. That little voice inside telling me, "Do not open to anyone that may laugh or judge you, keep quiet then you won't get hurt." If only I flipped that around and realized it didn't matter what anyone else thought of me, but I was too young to see.

Those days within the class room I remember sitting at my desk terrified at the mention of my name being called upon to participate. Class participation was the scariest thing for me which may seem so unusual to others, but this was who I was. I wanted to be invisible and wished often I could pull out an invisibility cloak to wrap around myself, to not be seen. Of course, there is no such thing but that didn't stop me wondering if it was possible to invent one somehow. I did try, not to invent the cloak, but to be more visible, outgoing, but for the most part I just wanted the earth to open up and swallow me. The thought of reading for the class, standing out in front, sharing any part of myself with others was terrifying for me. Embarrassment levels 100/100.

We are taught at school that we have to be outgoing but some of us don't fit in that mold. We all have different qualities and strengths; we are not all the same. We learn differently, we think differently, we function differently. What fits for one child may not fit for another.

"Everybody is a Genius – but if you judge a fish by its ability to climb a tree it will live its whole life believing it is stupid."

– Albert Einstein

Chapter 5
Missing Pieces

The depth of that missing piece as time moved on became increasingly stronger, I guess because I was getting older. When I was younger and more open to my energy friend, the missing piece was faint, as I became older and shut down more, the void deepened. The yearning, seeking, desire to find it became greater, feeling that I was now definitely a piece short of the puzzle. Hollowness within, emptiness, a longing for someone or something that I had no idea but just knew was missing. I was not a miserable child; I was pleasurably happy, but the scars I wore every day of wearing a mask covering up my true self was difficult for me. So when I needed to sit with myself, the real me, I did, as I needed this time alone to fully reconnect to my true self.

I would sneak away to the bushland across from my home. We had built a makeshift tree cubby house that consisted of an old blue car (bench) seat and a few other bits and pieces. I wasn't keen on spiders or snakes; they freaked me out, but I didn't really think about what may be lurking around. Just sitting there alone, the two of us – my energy friend and me along with the sounds of silence. I guess today I know it as meditation but back then I didn't, it was just something I knew I needed and the feeling just came natural. These times together in the trees, away from everyone else, I felt completely comfortable to openly chat to my friend. Again I could hear the words so loud and clear, and I felt free to laugh with him, answer him, ask him questions to seek answers where I felt lost, and just embed myself in this energy for as long as I could. My energy friend's guidance was invaluable to me, his words priceless, his love heavenly, and for a little girl I waited on every breath to hear him talk to me, hear his responses, hear his laugh and feel so close to him once again. I cherished these moments; these were the moments that connected us back together so strongly. I realized even more in these times that it was never him that faded away, it was me.

Being in the tree house probably wasn't the safest plan in retrospect, sitting there physically as one alone, but I always felt protected. I wasn't really sure what my friend would do if someone did try to hurt me, if someone was lurking in the bush or passing by and saw me, but I was assured they would know if anyone was approaching and tell me we need to leave. After all, they could see everything. From a physical perspective, there wasn't much he could do really. Protecting someone while not in physical form would be a little difficult I'd imagine, but again, I never stopped to think about that before I ventured off on my own.

My bedroom was another place I would sit in silence, sometimes just laying on my bed gathering my thoughts or usually feeling into my heart. For a little girl, I had a cute room with the usual set up, along with a small blue writing desk, a timber book shelf for my weird and strange books, and a night light. I had to have a light; I wasn't comfortable in darkness. I had pictures on my wall like most pre-teens that I had pulled out of magazines or any other place I saw them. They were usually of my favorite bands, singers, or surfers. I didn't buy them from shops; I wasn't really into spending money on things I could obtain for free. I had no idea about brand names or expensive toys and devices although I did buy records of course, but we made up our own mixed recorded cassette tapes to listen to. I was not a materialistic child in any way; I loved the simplicity of life. My bedroom had wide glass doors leading out to our front balcony, which enabled me to step outside at night to watch the stars in the sky. I was fascinated with stars, how they twinkled, sparkled, and shone so bright and almost every time I was looking up at them I asked myself – what is really out there? And where did I really come from?

I used to feel I could fly up to the stars and look back down to earth, coming and going as I pleased. One day, I went a little too far jumping off the balcony thinking I may be able to fly. The consequence of that little escapade was very sore ankles and knees, and I was shocked actually that I wasn't injured far worse; I was definitely being protected that day.

I loved my bedroom with its calm ambiance, and I felt exceptionally grateful to have this sacred space.

As the years passed, I integrated further into this world and less into the other, living more in my mind and ego and less from my heart and soul. Feeling my energy friend less, pretending not to feel what was missing, and trying to fill that space with something else. Longing and searching to fill the void. I think I had an understanding deep in my heart that there was only one thing that could stop this feeling, but I was afraid to admit that, as I thought I was losing my love forever.

Something inside told me to start writing, it was the way for me to express what I had suppressed. It was the only way I felt I could speak, share, let it all out. So I asked Mum if she would buy me a diary, which she did, and writing became my savior. When I was alone in my room, reading, writing, or listening to music I felt the connection with my energy love more. When I was out with others or distracted, it was faint. Some days, when the love was like this, I wondered if this would be the day he left me for good, or will he keep walking with me? Am I too old now? Was there an expiration date?

To me, if they left, I would be shattered, although the unbelievable euphoric love and protection till now had me feeling extremely lucky and forever grateful. I was hoping he wouldn't leave me, it wasn't time. This incredible love I would miss, and to be honest I wasn't that old. So why couldn't he just hang around, especially, if he wasn't coming in to the physical world to be with me. When I felt my friend, my face would light up, my whole being was alive again, my light shone like a beacon, and it was like food for my soul. I could never really explain to the depths of how it felt so blissfully magical. It would wash over me like the perfect wave, and suddenly, in that moment, I was elated, everything was love, flawless, light, powerful, whole, and I would be in my element.

Those early years now were starting to fade a little, as I concentrated less on myself and more on fitting in. I had two framed quotes hanging on my wall and that pretty much summed up how I felt about life. One was the famous '*Footprints in the sand*' which is a poem known to many, and the other was a picture of a beautiful sunny day with a little girl picking a flower, the quote read:

'It's a beautiful day, now watch someone come along and stuff it up.'

Reading between the two, you could tell that I was quite confused about life and what it was all about. On one hand, I had this supernatural love and energy experience; and on another, there always seemed to be something difficult to deal with. Such profound quotes for a child to have on her wall, but it depicted the two halves of me.

Summer Holidays

The summer was upon us, and I couldn't be happier. Summer days were spent at the beach, which was situated at a walking distance from our home. Beach chairs, umbrellas, food and beverages, days of swimming, and having fun in the sun. We would gather up all our supplies to head out walking to the beach, only two streets away, and we were there. Our front bay beach was lined with different colored beach boxes, some built from brick others from timber, some painted with multi-colors, some striped, and some plain. Usually the owners of these boxes would be at the beach themselves, opening them up to bring out their canoes, little boats, and more; so they could go out on the water. We would secure our umbrellas in the sand; our little beach chairs underneath out of the direct sunlight, and lay out the towels. Buckets and spades to make sandcastles would come out next, and we would all be set for the day. When the tide was out, we would walk out to the sand bars to play, which seemed like miles from the shore because the water was so shallow. People back on the sand looked a bit like ants. After several hours, at the beach – laughing, playing, and having lots of fun – we would pack everything up and head home again. I loved those days at the beach and those warm summer nights where we would just relax on our deck. Summer holidays – a time when I could be myself, and I didn't have to try so hard.

Our summer holidays were only six weeks in Australia, but I always made the most of them till the last day. However, this particular summer was a bit more memorable than most, with my brother accidentally smashing me in the face with a wooden totem tennis bat whilst playing and breaking my nose... *OUCH!* Did he swing back too hard? Or did I walk out our back door being too close and into the bat, who knew? (That was a debatable topic for some time) Not that it really mattered. It was such a shock, and at first, my mum didn't think it was broken, however, I ended up in hospital having surgery three days later, and they had to break my nose again to reconstruct it. I was 11 years old and wondered what hit me. My brother did, of course, feel terrible and there were many jokes made about how he came to hit me in the nose with the bat, however, it was completely misjudged and an accident. I couldn't really see the funny side of it at the time whilst I was in incredible pain, blood pouring down my face, and a smashed in nose, having surgery and healing with plaster on my face. But I do see the funny side of it today. Because it was smashed up quite bad, it required a cast, and I had to walk around with this cast for four weeks.

How embarrassing, the shy girl that already got embarrassed at the smallest things. It wasn't really my prettiest sight, and those summer beach days I was so excited about – went out the window.

I didn't really feel like going out or mixing with others much that summer; I rather stayed home, so I made the best out of what I called an embarrassing situation and was grateful that's all that got broken. Because it was my face, I could still do most things, and there was always my beloved music and dance. The nice beach days, I was looking forward to though, were not very enticing anymore and of course. I couldn't get my face wet. But I have always believed that things happen for a reason, and nothing by chance. Perhaps, the universe was guiding me to spend more time at home, indoors, this summer to feel more connected to my friend.

With my summer beach days now gone, leaving me to find other activities, it seemed like a good time to learn to play the piano. My mother was a beautiful pianist; and from the time I was a little girl, I would sit next to her and watch her play. It took me to places and beyond, as her music echoed through the house. I had never desired to play despite my mum trying several times to teach me, as she encouraged us to learn an instrument, but now it was time. Guitar was my first choice to learn, but I didn't possess one of those, however, I did have an amazing piano in my home so, 'piano' it was. Mum was truly gifted, and the way her fingers glided across those keys so elegantly was beautiful. Both my brother and I would follow in her footsteps. It didn't take me long to pick it up; we were both naturals and before long I was playing without music; and in that summer, my piano days were born.

Chapter 6
Walk with Me

Opening my eyes, staring up to my bedroom ceiling, all I could think was:

Today has arrived.

Pulling myself out of bed and pressing my feet firmly onto the carpet, a million thoughts were flashing through my head. As I drew back my orange floor to ceiling curtains (orange because of the '70s of course), I admired this beautiful sunshine streaming through into my room. I sat back down on my bed gazing out the window, and I wondered – *would he walk with me today?* As this thought came to mind, I checked in to see if I could I feel my love energy with me? I closed my eyes and connected to myself. He was instantly with me, immediately, as I connected his energy was fully present. I could feel him so deep within my heart and soul. I spoke the words and asked him from my heart for extra guidance to get through today. I knew he would be there because he had never failed me before. Still, today, I was nervous, anxious, and afraid. This was the first day of a new adventure, and one I had been dreading. As I reached out to touch him, like I had many times before, I asked him to please "Come be with me?" This wasn't new; I had asked him many times before, but today I tried again, desperate and hoping he could magically appear. Of all the times I had asked, today was a day I really needed him. I prayed to God (although I didn't see god as most religious folk did); I prayed to that higher presence, higher power, God source to please bring my energy friend in my world with me now. We had done this 'me in this world, him in another' thing way too long, it was time!

Maybe I didn't believe in my heart enough that it could happen, or maybe it just wasn't his time to be with me, I didn't know; but either way, it seemed I was on my own today.

Leaving my room to head downstairs so preoccupied by my own thoughts, I almost overlooked our pet magpie 'Maggie', tapping on the glass doors of the dining room with its beak for breakfast. As I opened the door to hand feed him some meat (his daily choice), which he gladly accepted, our rather large, ginger pussycat 'Ginger' rushed inside for his morning feed as well. (Yes, I know we weren't really thinking outside the box when we named those two). As much as I was preoccupied, the nerves were still present, and I was in silence.

Every young person gets nervous about this day; except I was nervous for a different reason, and I prayed my energy friend would stay and help me. I was a quiet shy girl about to step into her first day at high school with hundreds of other youth I'd never seen before; this was so daunting for me. Yes, I was the talkative girl around friends and family I was comfortable with. But when it came to spreading my wings with strangers, that was a different story, and we already knew how my school days had fared so far. How many masks would I have to wear to get through this day and the days to come? The thought of it was unimaginable.

There's a saying when you start high school that most of us have heard. You're going from 'a big fish in a small pond, to a little fish in a big pond'. This was an excellent way of describing the transformation from primary to secondary education. Well, I felt like *'a tadpole in a river'*. Yep, it was not in any way exciting or fun for me. It only signified I had to now layer more masks to fit in at school, and if I wasn't good at that, I would be subjected to judgment and bullying that I could no longer avoid. I had been subjected to what I would call 'light' name calling and bullying in my final year of Primary school (because I was a loner and different), and I'd prayed this wouldn't follow me. But for what I felt I could handle in my past school, I knew this was the big league, here I wasn't so sure. I felt further under the microscope and the only thing remotely making this experience any better was my brother still being school. It was a nice feeling; but in these times, it was sort of 'fight your own battles' don't get your big brother to fight them for you. It was a relief to know he was there to protect me if needed, but let's be honest, who wants their little sister hanging around when you're in senior levels. If I had any hope of this not following me, I would have to basically re-invent myself as a different person. Pretend to be more extroverted. I could attest first hand that introverts were generally not really accepted too kindly in school.

Over the summer, I had introduced myself to reading *'Dolly'* magazine. It was a 'girls' best friend and go to magazine that pretty much taught us anything we needed to know. I had toyed with the idea of how I was to learn more about being a teenager – although I was not one quite yet! I read every inch of the copies I could get my hands on, so I felt a little more equipped on my first day in the big pond, *'or the ocean'* and right there and then *'Dolly'* became 'My Bible'.

(*The gratitude I have for that magazine – no one will ever know. I cannot thank 'Dolly' magazine enough; I grew up with Dolly and it was my saving grace*).

Not only was I an exceptionally shy girl, I was also just far too embarrassed to talk to anyone about personal private matters, that would extend to matters of the heart as well. Getting up close and personal with another was not in me. Deep and meaningful conversations with another just exposed way to much of whom I was and what I had learnt to hide for many years. I'm not saying this was a good thing, but it was someone I had become.

My mother was quite a shy introverted lady and kept things to herself too; she never really discussed the more deep and meaningful topics. As much as our family were close in other ways, we kept the much deeper emotions to ourselves.

The only one I was happy to get up close and personal with was my beautiful spirit energy friend who knew me better than I knew myself. In every way, he knew every intricate detail, feeling, emotion, and fear about me. It was like having a person inside you, being completely transparent but it wasn't uncomfortable at all. I know it's hard to imagine how we could ever be so totally ourselves and natural whilst being fully transparent, but it was easy. Being completely vulnerable and having him see the *real* me, my complete truth along with all of my flaws being exposed, was not scary for me. It wasn't scary because he felt like home to me *every day* in *every way*. So, really, it was just like being with myself.

Consequently, *'Dolly'* was what got me through the ups and downs of growing up in a physical world, and *'Dolly'* would get me through many peer pressure moments.

My height and looks, (as I looked older for my age) plus my maturity, gave the appearance I was somewhat older than a new comer starting high school. So I didn't have trouble actually fitting in with that regard. However, being in a crowded school was intimidating with very little to no privacy. I had entered the closest Co-Ed school which was one of the largest in the district and with so many students. I felt I was on display. I'm pretty sure no one was paying any attention to me, but regardless, I wanted to be invisible. The up side was being around older youth. If I had to fit in or find friends, older people were who I was most comfortable with. So in a way as much as there was nervousness being dropped at that school gate, there was also anticipation of mingling with older teens.

I was a creature of habit, meaning whatever I felt comfortable with I did. I stayed in the same areas, hung out with the same people, hid myself at the back of the class, and hoped the teacher forgot my name. I thought if I could wish myself to be invisible then maybe the teacher would think I was to. (No cloak this time)

If I walked into a class and the teacher said, "Let's change seats all the people at the back sit at the front and vice versa." I literally wanted to die, that's how painful being noticed or speaking in front of others was for me. I actually was known to skip a class if I knew in advance that was happening. I'm sure the teachers thought this was helping kids like me, but it wasn't. It was absolutely not helping me in any way to come out of my shell. Being forced or pushed to do something wasn't the way. I cannot begin to even explain how those school days were so incredibly difficult for me. There were rare occasions that I felt comfortable with a teacher and the possibility of speaking up, and this made my school days more bearable, but there weren't many of those classes. Even when I felt super confident and was performing well academically, I still wanted to hide.

Unless you are introverted and shy, having also experienced these situations, it most probably seems absurd to others who are so outgoing, they can't fathom such a thing, but it is very much real to us.

"What we resist – persists.
If you are resisting being yourself, you will persist to have
problems. You will never create a living, only an existing.
Never really shine in the world or live from your true passion
and purpose, heart and soul. You will merely cycle through
life, escaping one fear only to fall into another – What we
resist persists."
Be your true self!

When you think about it how 'super cool' was it, (yes, I had the *'Slang'* down pat now) to share my life with a beautiful loving energy. When I thought about it, how lucky was I to have this protector – best friend, guide, unconditional love – all to myself. He was mine, and I was his. How many people had that? I knew I was still so blessed to have him.

Maybe in today's society, I might have had a line of teenagers queued up around the classrooms to have a metaphysical conversation, perhaps, even a psychic reading, but back then I would have been called nuts. I guess even today there are still some ignorant people in society that would say that, but I love to think we have traveled significantly further in our level of consciousness and perception of the world we live in today.

So if you are reading this, and you are a kid like me, don't be afraid to be yourself, and don't be afraid to be different or called nuts. I regret I didn't take on my title and be myself, but mostly I regret hiding my beautiful energy friend. Hiding him meant I was not honoring us, a special privilege I was given upon my incarnation to this world and one that 'despite' how many times I tried to squash or hide, sabotage it to be honest, it never left. He remained walking with me, unconditionally loving me. How many people can honestly say they not only had that privilege, but they knew it?

Despite all of this, the first year was panning out not quite as painful in secondary school as I imagined. Although I might have counted down the hours from that first period bell, I adapted in a way that was semi-comfortable. I wore the masks I needed to; I didn't mention anything about my energy friend (which didn't make me feel nice) or the fact I felt different. My way of telling people how different I felt was just by saying I was painfully shy, and I avoided every single situation that could result in any sort of embarrassment. Of course, sometimes, it was unavoidable. Circumstances would creep up on me when I least expected, but I pretended to fit in as best I could.

I befriended a nice girl in the year level above me pretty early in the year. We seemed to connect well, and I really enjoyed her company. She was an only child and quite mature for her age. I would say she was probably my first ever close friend I'd had. However, on so many levels the effort I went to not expose myself, to avoid possible ridicule, was ridiculous and a waste of time. As humans, we so often adapt according to what makes us as comfortable as possible, and we suppress the rest in fear of other's opinions – instead of accepting ourselves. Although I moved through school with this demeanor, surprisingly, my grades where above average. I excelled in Mathematics, Science and Prac classes with top marks and with all other subjects producing B's. I think being an old soul and the feeling of having done this many times before helped. I possibly was tapping into my higher wisdom at times as the education felt familiar, and let's face it, as we've noticed the system hasn't changed that much. Somewhere inside, I felt that I had already learnt all this before and if so, there must be a way to recall that. If I chose to spend more time 'tapping in' to my wisdom and being my true self, rather than exerting all my energy on covering up, perhaps, I could have been genius status!

My energy friend walked with me at school; although it was faint, and several times. I was too caught up in my acting skills, playing out the role I had created for myself to fully feel his presence. Nonetheless, being a quiet student allowed me to go within myself more and feel him, and even without doing that I could see I was receiving his help. Many days when uncomfortable situations arose, I asked. *Where are you? I need assistance,* but sometimes instead of trusting him to help, my fear and panic would take over a situation and then I was completely lost in my mind to even feel him or anything within.

In my opinion, meditation time should become compulsory in every education facility throughout the world, even if it's only ten minutes. Oh, how the world would be a different place if this was implemented. I had no idea what meditation was or its incredible benefits at this age, but it certainly would have made my life a lot easier. I was a girl that needed meditation, quiet, and to learn to be balance and centered. I had been doing some form of this throughout my life but to fully understand and practice it daily would have been beneficial in producing a positive impact on my life.

Sex-Ed

Turns out my '*Dolly*' magazines whilst saving the day, had some tough competition when I discovered sex education had been introduced being compulsory to attend. Well that was just fantastic! How would I cope with this? Truthfully, this could have certainly been a test for me, but I was happy when I saw our teacher. The class was conducted by a very compassionate open minded teacher that was extremely gentle and understanding whilst conveying this topic, I would say though '*Dolly*' magazine still had the edge. As uncomfortable it must feel for the teacher looking out to a sea of naïve uncomfortable faces, that awkward moment when she or he starts to discuss the intricate details of reproduction, sexual anatomy, and safe sex, I can assure you it's just as uncomfortable for us. It's a bit sad though we all feel this way and find it difficult to express such a vulnerable subject. Sexuality had long been a 'taboo' topic, but it had become more openly discussed since the '60s sexual revolution. We were not there yet, but it was progressing, having it introduced to early levels of high school education was showing progress. The seemingly 'off limits' forbidden conversation that had carried a 'dirty sinful' type energy for generations was now starting to evolve. However, sex conversations with your parents were still as awkward and embarrassing as it ever was, so these classes became an excellent replacement. Sitting far, removed from the front row as I possibly could (which means I rushed to the back of the classroom), I thought I'll be fine if the teacher doesn't ask me any questions, which thank god they didn't. Safe to say, I breezed through sex education and actually quite enjoyed the experience.

Piano classes started following on from my mother's summer teachings, as she wanted me to learn from a professional. I was absolutely okay for her to remain teaching me, but she insisted. So I went along once a week on Wednesday nights after school to piano class. I *was* very fortunate with piano having natural talent, I could pick up and memorize the music very quickly only needing to play it once and it was not forgotten. I became an exceptionally quick learner, and my brother was the same. We both continued to take lessons for a while until our mum gave us the choice a year later to finish classes if we weren't passionate about learning anymore. I wished I made the choice to keep going as playing the piano is a beautiful skill, but for some reason, it didn't seem *'cool'* to play the piano, so I gave up. Once again I allowed the current **trend** to overshadow my desires, but at the time, I was trying painfully to be accepted and fit in, and I never knew many that were learning piano.

My mother always did things she wanted to do from her heart; she never worried about who else was doing them or if it was popular. I saw this amazing gift in her and wished I had the courage to do the same, but somehow it got lost on me. We exert an incredible amount of energy on trying to be like all others when again, *why can't we see that it's beautiful to be different?*

By this stage, though I had played on stage at a concert in front of hundreds, it was a bit nerve racking for me, needless to say that was my one and only time, but I continued to play piano at home and taught myself easily. My first major piece I learnt to play was a beautiful song, a rather haunting piece from a movie every bit the same *'The Rose'* by Bette Midler. This movie loosely depicted the life story of the late singer Janis Joplin. I didn't know who she was, but I learnt she was a famous 1960s singer who inspired with her raw bluesy sound. Her passion for music along with its lifestyle took its tool, and at 27 years of age, she died of an accidental overdose. The movie was quite depressing but it touched my heart so deeply, I had no idea why and may still not, but I feel it had a lot to do with who she wanted to be but couldn't.

In school, I quickly adapted to my favorite places and discovered I was your typical Science nerd; I couldn't get enough of anything science related. Understanding energy, atoms, chemicals and reactions, waves, motions, metals, biotechnology, electricity, the list went on. Chemical experiments I could do all day and when the teacher started talking Bunsen burners I was in my element, very few things excited me at school, however, Bunsen Burners did. It was the only time of the day I was upset to hear the end of the period bell because science was my thing. Could I just have six periods of science each day please?! Unfortunately, no, I couldn't. But for some reason, it felt close to home for me. I resonated with it all so well. Not much in this life to this point was making any sense to me, but my science classes were. I was a happy girl feeling at home in the science lab.

Home time would arrive by the sound of the bell, *ohhhhh* did I love that sound in last period. A quick exit, bus trip, and fast walk home equaled more time after school for dancing and remixing music with my brother each night. We spent more time on music and choreography routines rather than our homework. My brother was one of the smartest people I knew, he excelled in all areas, and I was so proud to have him as my big brother. School was a breeze for him, always receiving top marks, but I never felt I had to compete at all, my parents just always encouraged me to be an individual, to do my best and be myself (not that I was being the latter) so never did I really feel pressured. The only time, perhaps, was when I was assigned a teacher that had already taught him, and they expected me to be as smart.

We both continually surprised our mother at our ability to spend an hour in front of the Television, whilst being able to multi task watching our favorite program accomplishing our homework in record time with half our concentration, still achieving top results. She would say to us:

"Imagine how amazing you both could do if you turned *off* the Television and studied in quiet, actually, using your full concentration."

(She had a point, and we thought about it for a while, but not for too long)

So then we would explain:

"It's all good Mum, we are getting good grades why change the system!"

And what could she say to that, she would roll her eyes and walk out of the room. I don't think she had a good enough comeback that was going to give her a win on this subject.

Combining our dance and music talents, my brother stepped things up to start making dance music movies with our newly bought movie camera. He developed a passion for film so the screen, projector, tripod, and camera were always set up in our upstairs living area ready to go. This was my happy place; they were happy times, seeing our talents and dancing techniques on screen was fun. Filming wasn't exclusive to these either, often there would be a camera pointed at our face; he was always filming, cutting, editing, and capturing magic moments for the screen. At the conclusion of our week, our family would sit down for a movie night to watch his masterpieces, sometimes with surprise. (How he never ended up being a filmmaker or DJ is beyond me!)

An important lesson I had learnt throughout my life from a seven-year-old was that you can't just keep laying masks, being someone you're not, to avoid judgment or scrutiny. Eventually, it messes with who you really are because you've spend too much time trying to be someone else, and before you know it, everything you knew to be or who you truly are starts to slip away. I was damaging the very situation I was so privy too, a unique beautiful experience. A love so magical that I was shutting out because I was hiding from myself, which meant I was hiding from my energy connection.

I needed to find someone that understood, that was aware and conscious like me to talk to, but finding a likeminded soul in my area wasn't easy. The conscious movement was escalating around the globe like I said, but nobody was sharing it around me. Or so I thought. *How I wished for that something missing to be present in my physical reality.*

The End of an Era...'70s... How We Saw It

...it was the end of the '70s and was it a colorful decade to remember. It brought with it Hippies reeling from the late '60s with a lot of colored clothing, way out patterns, swirls, and wild designs. Orange was the leading color of choice, but that didn't exclude the lime greens, browns, and gold. People entered into a different lifestyle with Disco clubs, dance studios, alcohol, drugs, and more. This decade was early for me, so I was way too young to participate in any of this; however, I was a huge fan of the disco genre throughout and was happy it stayed around.

Pet Rocks (yes, you heard right, and yes I had one!) Mood rings and water beds made an appearance, whilst crystals, incense, bean bags, and the funky Swag lamps everyone seemed to have. Lava lamps were popular too, and I think we all had one of those clock radios with large white numbers that we could hear clicking over each time. Clogs were fashionable. While down under in Australia, someone had invented a shoe called 'Treads', they were made from tire treads with weaved suede sandal look, very surfie, extremely hippie. I loved them but my mum wouldn't buy me a pair because she thought they were too old for me. However, one day my aunt handed down her old pair to me, and I thought it was Christmas. Avocado Green with black markings, they were way too big but it didn't stop me thinking I was *'super cool'.*

The yellow smiley face saying 'have a nice day' appeared on many things from T-shirts, to bumper stickers, quickly escalating around the world sharing the bright and happy.

We had women's Liberation, Vietnam War, and many other wars throughout the decade in various countries. I didn't really understand any of the political agenda influence or incidents of the '70s being so young, but even if I had been old enough, I'm not sure I would have engaged or expressed an opinion. Even as a very young girl, it all looked like a bit of a mess. It was easy to escape the fear around it all, as we didn't have the media streaming the drama into our living rooms like today. I knew I was truly blessed to be living in a country where none of that really affected us at all, although I am aware that others around the world were not so lucky. However, in 1975 when Australia had finally fazed in color TV, it was to have a huge impact. Many now were taking more notice, and I felt our innocence started to slip away.

Although we could see what was going on in the world, I have to say my life compared to that was a bit like *The Brady Bunch*, well minus all the kids and Alice. Plus mum never got dressed up in her special dresses with accompanying high heel shoes to cook dinner or dust the furniture, but you get my point. On that note *The Brady Bunch* I could now watch in color, along with everything else. *Bewitched*, *Happy days*, *The Adams Family*, *I dream of Jeannie,* and *Gilligan's island* were usually my top choices growing up.

Other milestone events throughout this decade included the split of *The Beatles*." Epic movies *Star Wars* and *Jaws* invaded our screens, whilst *Saturday Night Fever* was a Disco Phenomenon, including music from our very own 'Bee Gees'. Grease followed with record breaking figures and gave us all a taste of the '50s. It had girls considering whether they rather be a 'Sandra Dee' or 'Rizzo'. As much as I loved this movie to the moon and back, the end confused me a little when they flew off into the sky. The first video arcade game 'Space Invaders' was launched and beautiful Elvis Presley had died on the 16th of August, 1977 leaving my mum devastated. That day will always be a memorable one; I can still remember where I was and what I was doing when that news entered our household. As I was coming down our staircase, I could hear my mother cry out, "Elvis has died, Elvis has died," she was crying and so distraught, I asked her what happened and she told me what had been reported. Elvis' death created frenzy throughout the world with people rushing to record shops to buy his records, newspapers pumping out extra editions to report the latest, and people all around the world were devastated at the death of the 'king of rock and roll'. I think most would still remember today where they were when they got that news.

The Boeing 747 made its debut. Australia hosted its first Mardi Gras in Sydney, and although this was met with police violence, it was a major civil rights milestone, along with a message to many that *as always* 'Love has no boundaries!'. Technology was fully seen for the first time in many ways. Microsoft was founded on my birthday in '75, Apple computers were launched along with email and floppy disks, and the Walkman was popular. We had the first release of Beta VCR tapes; they were funny looking things but to be able to tape a show and re-watch when you desired was a trip. Of course, there were plenty of other events that occurred throughout this time, some I have already mentioned, and plenty I haven't.

Overall the '70s were fairly kind for a girl that was finding her way in a world she was so unattached to, whilst feeling attached to another. For living in a world that seemed so foreign with confusion of not being able to be herself, it wasn't a bad decade to navigate through. (Thank god for music is all I can say). We did have many joyous occasions, and my energy love was there traveling the '70s with me – even when at times I thought he may have left, but without a doubt he was with me always and still is. As the years passed, I had grown layering the masks where necessary on the outside, but on the inside, I was still me. To my family, I'm sure they still saw the quirky shy me; and to the outside world, I was someone else. To my energy friend, I felt joined with such pure love, he got to see every part of me truthfully, whilst helping and guiding me through those years.

Chapter 7
The '80s Had Arrived

It was now the '80s and things had started to change. I had started working when I turned 12 at my local convenience store having now been there a year. But the fact I was now a teenager and needed some more funds, I thought it may be a good idea to start looking for a new job that paid a little higher. I had come to the conclusion that it was time for an upgrade and change of employment, so off I went looking. This was a time that roller skating was super cool (yes, I said it, 'super cool') and extremely popular, so what better place to start than our newly built roller skating center close to my home. So I applied for a job and, much to my surprise, I got it. I had to spend a few weeks training at another center, as we needed to be trained in a few different areas but then I was to start at our center on opening day. It was all quite new to me, and I had to learn a lot, but I was excited for the change. My new job was a walking distance from my home which was great, as I didn't need to rely on my parents to take me to work, I could walk there myself in ten minutes. Skating was a fun place to be, as it didn't require parental supervision, so it was kind of like a little getaway on your own to explore and have some fun. The rink was opposite the beach which gave us that lovely sea breeze, plus the added bonus of crossing the road to sit by the water on your work breaks. Skating was filled with good music, fun times and junk food (my favorite was hot dogs) with the advantage that if you didn't want to talk to anyone you could make a quick escape onto the rink if needed. I actually liked just skating around on my own, as it gave me time to secretly be with my energy friend, well in a way, as he was more faint in these times when I was out because I was preoccupied, but I could still feel something with him which was better than nothing at all.

I loved to skate!

I could be in my own little world, actually being in there felt like it was another world, *and you know how I felt about that*. But seriously, I became a bit of a roller skating junkie also, taking lessons. I learned to do jumps, turns, and spins (which made me dizzy), and I'm not really sure why I felt the need to do this because I had no intention of entering competitions, perhaps, it was just my creative dance moves extending onto wheels, but I did enjoy it at the time. Once I achieved all my badges, I stopped having lessons, as I was satisfied with my skills.

One thing I'd overlooked though with this new position was that I had to talk and serve a lot more people than my previous employment. Not an easy thing to do when you're shy, plus try serving every kid you know from school and them watching you do your job. For me, it turned out to be quite nerve racking. So on went another mask! It's funny, though, because many times I worked on my own when I was in the kiosk, and although I was busy, I felt I had someone helping me. It would be the most random times I was flat out and quickly looking for new stock or trying to get the popcorn machine working and instead of becoming overwhelmed, I didn't, because it was like I was being helped, like someone was taking over and leading me. Some nights after we closed those doors, it would all start to sink in, just how busy I was on my own, how I coped and managed perfectly, and I would just shake my head thinking how on earth did I do that. I wondered many times if he was helping me, not that I had to really wonder that much. I knew he had given his protection since I was a little girl, that he was always there continually protecting and helping me.

One of the bonuses of working in a place like this at my age was seeing lots of nice boys. I had started to realize I was becoming more interested but way too shy to talk to any, unless it was talking about popcorn and hotdogs and handing over money. The perks for working at the rink were we could skate before opening hours with an empty rink so I used this time to get lost in myself whilst skating. Skating was my fun 'go to place', although one of the unsettling parts was the announcement of couples skating. With couples skating, you could get lucky and be asked, or you could end up feeling like a loser sitting on the sidelines watching all the other couples skating around. It was like a scene from a teen movie, the hot guys and pretty girls together and the rest hoping someone would skate up and take their hand. I never looked at myself as pretty or definitely not one of the popular girls. So did I spend more time getting lucky or being the loser? I may just keep this little secret to myself, but let's just say overall I fared better than average.

As the decade started, it brought with it the continuation of 'Disco Fever' from the '70s, along with an interesting pop culture. It seemed like changes had happened virtually overnight. Disco, you either loved it or hated it. I absolutely loved disco as it was all upbeat pop dance music, and I loved to dance. *You can always dance to disco!!!* The emergence of many more genres was streaming through; and whilst I was still heavily into bands, I continued to enjoy different types of music. I would still get lost in what fed my soul, but I was starting to notice a diversity and energy with music that I had never felt before.

December of 1980 we lost John Lennon and on the 11th May, 1981, at just 36 years old, we lost our incredible Reggae singer/songwriter Bob Marley. Two artists using powerful messages through their music to reach, awaken, and inspire people all around the world. Their messages were many, about bringing equality within our human race, bringing love, peace, joy, and togetherness as one. Living in a peaceful world where race would be insignificant, and we all accept each other as equal. Many mourned the loss of these two great artists; however, we were forever grateful they had left us with their infectious music that touched our hearts, souls and spread love, hope, and peace, as well as hopefully awaken the sleeping for many years to come. John Lennon's song *'Imagine'* is a song that spells it all out *oh* so simply. For me, I could resonate with these lyrics, being caught between two worlds and knowing life on this planet was not meant to be this way. I knew he could feel similar. He had something else going on in his world of knowing like I had experienced for all of mine. Was it that some of us were here to show others and teach them the way it really was, or did some of us just never 'forget' the love where we came from. Like me with my energy friend, I felt from his lyrics he had experienced this type of love, the deep soul love I had traveled with all my life.

A spiritual love greater than anyone could imagine.

It appeared we both connected with something so rare in this life that most didn't remember. This brought me greater comfort and peace to see that I wasn't the only one.

Time had passed and it was feeling like I was going through a transition of some sort. I had always felt mature for my age, but the pressure of puberty, the changes occurring in my life, having to be *seen* more proved extremely difficult for me. I think it was the combination of school, work, getting older, having to blend in further than ever before as I was constantly around a lot of people. More than ever I needed my support, my beautiful love beside me that always picked me up through hard times and carried me, not just walked with me. My angel, my invisible friend, all the names I didn't know how to refer to him when I was younger. It didn't really matter to know *exactly* who we were together. How we belonged or why he was traveling with me, it was too beautiful to question. He was with me and that's all that mattered. Every day, in my heart I felt him, and whilst some days he felt less than others, I knew he was still there. He never really left. It was me embedding myself further into my mind and less into my soul that created my experience of feeling he was distant or, worse yet, had left me. From a little girl, I felt like I had wings behind me and some days the feeling was stronger than others and these days were no different, I would still often look around to see if I did, or who it was. I felt I could almost touch them – the energy was so connected, so close, but each time I looked, my physical eyes would see nothing, nothing but an empty space, and each time I would whisper, "Come be with me…please."

I asked myself why could I not see him if I could feel him. Why was his light not reaching my eyes? I could feel his incredible euphoric light shining so bright, but yet I was blind. I longed to see him, touch him, and feel him in physical form, but he wasn't here with me in his physical presence so it was impossible. In some supernatural way, I had a sense of what he would look like. Through a visualization that had come to me, I could almost see his smile and beautiful eyes. I didn't hear him speak, but somehow I heard what he might sound like if he spoke words. It was like he didn't need to speak for me to hear him, and he didn't need to tell me. He could speak his mind in such a profound way needing very few words to communicate. It was as real as if he was standing in front of me, as real as if I was able to reach out and touch him. This was new to me what I was being shown and it made me want him with me in physical form even more. When I was only very young, I could see my energy friend, until I couldn't. Now he was coming to me in a different form, showing me himself. As I held my hand out to touch him, I would see the image flash before me, but one I could not retain for any great time. It was fleeting. All I had was a split second if I was lucky, to glimpse this beautiful love guiding me. In all ways, I wished so deeply that he would appear before my eyes and be in this world with me. I was trying so hard to call him in, and had been since a little girl. Now I was a teenager and still asking him, I was starting to wonder if he would ever, or if his role was to stay in spirit with me.

Chapter 8
Teen Years

Given the changes I was going through, struggling to be more outgoing and fit in, it made me want to retreat to the very things that comforted and nurtured my authentic self – so I sought those very things that helped the most. Music feed my soul, it was therapy for me, and my passion for music had me a tad excited about MTV launching with our first 24-hour video music channel. It was kicking off with an already popular song *'Video Killed The Radio Star'* which had a rather interesting connotation to it. Some say this was not a coincidence, it was easy to see the irony and quite self-explanatory, I agreed. As for me, movie and TV celebrity pictures went up on my wall, I was keeping up with all the trends through 'my bible' it never missed a beat, and I was at the age now where I started to take notice of fashion. If we thought the '70s hairdos and colored clothing were far out, we were in for another surprise with the '80s. This was my era, and I loved the '80s, although it's highly possible some of my fellow '80s teens may not share my same enthusiasm.

It already felt at the beginning that it was going to be a somewhat decade to remember, changing the course of society as we knew it. The energy going into the '80s that I felt was difficult to explain, but it changed very quickly. I just wasn't keen on the fact that I still felt a bit like an alien. This feeling never left, still feeling like a square peg in a round hole, but I was attempting to fit in. There were some songs with pretty heavy lyrics about being lost and not fitting in that I was listening too, and I started to realize that I wasn't the only one after all. Perhaps, those penning the lyrics were not fitting in for different reasons than me, but just the same, they felt it. *'Fame'* was a favorite movie and when I first heard the song *'Out here on my own'* I was taken back, the lyrics I could very much relate to. I was always reaching for that guidance, help from an invisible energy presence that 'to others' made me look stupid. Did I feel stupid? Well not stupid because I knew I could feel more than others, but it did have its uniqueness, and therefore, could be difficult sometimes, especially, living in this social era.

This was a time when we started having lots of parties at our home. It was large enough to cater for many with the large living areas, and my parents loved bringing everyone together for some fun. We hosted birthdays, anniversaries, no excuse needed really; our home became the house that would host a party for any reason. We all truly loved to dance, and my brother was right at home being assigned as the DJ. Everyone loved his music/ mixes; he knew exactly the balance between genres and what the different age groups enjoyed hearing. These were the times when my 'rock and roll' jive days were born, as I would watch my parents in amazement at their dance skills. I wanted to learn to jive and thus my mum and dad taught me. My brother and I would showcase our choreographed pieces throughout the night and most joined in with us; we would dance until the early hours because no one wanted to go home. They all loved our parties. We brought a lot of laughs, fun, and enjoyment to all around us. My parents always had an abundance of food for all, and some friends would usually bring a prepared dish. Our buffet was the best party food spread you could imagine, and everyone got well excited over it.

My parents were average folk working multiple jobs to pay the bills, but their generosity for their friends and others astounded me. Even if they couldn't afford something they made it happen. If it was to cheer someone up, to help another, to be there, to lend them money they possibly couldn't spare, lend a car or anything, they were the kindest and most giving people I knew. My parents never judged, only helped. I will always have so much gratitude for having them as my parents.

I truly believe we are often put with families that understand us and ones that are here to help us achieve our life purpose. Without a doubt my family were meant for me, and I am ever so grateful.

As the decade progressed, radical changes were occurring and I don't just mean on the screen. Music and Technology were shifting at a rapid pace which was interesting for us as music fans. We still had a war (always had to have a war going on); Iran and Iraq this time. I was a teen that tried not to venture into conversations or acknowledgment 'despite my awareness' of worldly events. This drama created a fear vibration that took people away from love and happiness, although I was aware that we should be trying to help as well.

However, the early '80s years did have a strong political presence, and it was starting to become a bit doom and gloom, or maybe I was just getting a clearer picture of our planet that had gone unnoticed to me before. When we are young, we can stay naïve, or in our own little world but then as they say 'shit happens' and suddenly the exposure of such events etches its way a little further into your mind, bringing you a little further into the world of the Matrix.

In the face of this, I often still remained in my own world, doing my thing, trying to stay on the positive side of life. I'd rather choose to work out the fundamentals of the Rubik's Cube (which was a new invention) and stay in my music zone. Deep down in my heart, I knew I was brought into this world to promote love and kindness through my light, and maybe even through the light we both shared – my energy friend and me – because together 'let's face it' it was pretty awesome, and his pure love which he radiated through me, that set my soul on fire since I was a little girl – shared with others, would have produced some pretty amazing magic for those around us. I knew I wasn't here at all to get caught up in the negative side of life, the negative from others that seemed to spread far quicker than any positive. Ever noticed that? That the bad stuff spreads like wildfire but the good takes longer, *because it's harder to believe.* Why is it we believe and feed off the negative more, something to ask ourselves? Do we like the drama? Or are we simply just following along as a collective of sheep participating in the drama and hatred spread by others.

Perhaps, as I mentioned earlier, we have been shown through society's programming that it's bad to love ourselves and acceptable to not, acceptable to judge ourselves and listen to others. I don't believe there were too many amongst humanity that were so comfortable in their skin that they were living in their truth, me included. Again, it's easier to believe the bad stuff. How many of us believe the 'bad stuff' that feeds self-destructive thoughts. I'm too fat, I'm too thin, I'm so dumb, I'm ugly, I'm a freak, I'm different, I'm a loser, I'm an airhead, then comes the he's/she's better than me because… And the list goes on. It doesn't take long before lack of confidence and low self-esteem sets in, along with the judgment and hatred of oneself. Throw in a euphoric loving energy friend walking with you plus old soul living between two worlds and life definitely becomes interesting, to say the least.

On the upside I managed to solve fairly quickly, one thing that most of the world couldn't – the Rubik's cube! You could say that boosted my confidence more than a touch. It was a time where I didn't think a lot of myself due to how different I was. Sometimes, I needed the encouragement. However, when you put things into perspective, it was a bit sad that solving the Rubik's cube had to pose as my catalyst for feeling better within myself.

When you're not 'Hip'…but need to be prepared

We had a whole new language I had to learn now that we were in the '80s if I had any hope of fitting in. Peer pressure was upon me, upon all my age, and unless you could live in a rainforest or on a deserted island you didn't have much choice. New slang words had been born with the *'80s.* I'm not sure what was wrong with the others I had already learnt in the '70s, but as time moves on it becomes 'daggy' to say such words and new 'cooler or Rad' words become the new vocab.

So everyone quickly started sprouting 'totally Rad' that's 'lame' or 'she's an airhead', (lucky I wasn't called that) well not to my face anyway. 'Dude' became popular and 'total babe'. You got 'sprung' if you got caught and were a 'total spaz'. 'Tubular', 'grody', and 'stoked' were popular (not really with me) with words like 'mint', 'wicked', "sweet', and 'ace' always used (those more me). 'Bite me' (I tended to use this more regularly) being in 'deep shit', which 'sucked' was a 'classic'. When someone got surprised it was 'Wowser', and if they didn't believe you it was 'give me a break' or 'are you legit'. The one I didn't particularly like if you seemed different was 'freak' I thought for sure I might get labeled with that one, although surprising enough I never did, well again, to my face anyway. 'To the max' was one I used a lot and of course we didn't always speak the language, but one was to learn in case one was having a conversation where these phrases were used, so one could have an understanding of what the hell they were talking about. Once again 'my bible' had already caught me up to speed on most but it was handy to learn a few more. Being in Australia, we often got things a little later, but in another way we were on top of it since we watched more American Television than Australian. I was now armed and ready not looking like a fool if I got caught off guard; because if you slipped up, you could be sure to be laughed at, or if you didn't get what someone was indicating you were such a 'loser'. So let's just make sure we got it right!

Although it had it's fun element at the time – the things we thought we had to do to fit in, I know, it looks ridiculous when you read it like that, but alas most of the world operates this way no matter what decade you're from.

At school, I still traveled under the radar as much as possible, still producing good grades and trying to stay in the back of the class. Computers had been introduced with our generation, and in Australia, we had the introduction of them in our high schools when I started. We didn't have one at home, most families didn't at this early stage, but we now had a whole subject called computer studies designed for us to learn all about this new technology. The programming was not as easy to learn as they are now, and very different computers to what we use today. We had no World Wide Web – no internet, we couldn't just 'google' for the answer or have an online encyclopedia before our eyes. We still had to research and read books; libraries were still in full swing. We carried books not

USB sticks, and it was quite a bit heavier to carry our bags to and from school. If you had an argument with someone it was in person. There was no jumping onto their social media page to hide behind cyber bullying. If you were having a relationship with someone you actually had to speak to them, and if you were not in the presence of another your only option was your home phone.

Each day I still felt lost at school, I had this sort of side to me that was a true 'Aries' female. I was independent, strong, creative, determined, and my 'old soul' wisdom was active each moment. But my shyness and desire to be invisible and for everyone to just leave me alone and my fear of being judged was at the forefront. Again, it was like living between two parts of myself.

I wondered how many other teenagers may be feeling similar to how I did.

I was extremely uncomfortable around boys and no idea why. I didn't really want a boyfriend although I was curious; however, the thought of being that close to another scared me. What if he sees into my soul, would he see the real me and how far would I have to open my true self and my heart up to him. Would I be exposed? This all appeared to be far too much for me, so I avoided males at all costs. They didn't always avoid me, though, so dodging boys at school became another obstacle. Whilst I felt like this I longed for a male friend to talk too, not be in a relationship with, but to have as a friend. I considered myself too young *in age – not maturity* for a boyfriend, and boys don't have all the bitchiness and drama that girls do. I wasn't into any of the female bitchiness or drama, so I preferred a boy as a friend. However, I noticed boys don't really want to just be friends they always seem to have a hidden agenda. Well, in my experience, they did. Perhaps, boys are designed this way, perhaps, they don't see themselves as being able to have a 'girl' as a best friend, although I had seen it play out this way in television shows but maybe that was just for the purpose of the script, because in real life looking around I couldn't see this in my world. As soon as you became friends or close with a boy 'as a friend', everyone was quick to see you as 'together' – boyfriend and girlfriend, and nobody really believed you if you did say you were just friends. This was not my experience, but I had observed this at my school several times, and it appeared when boys were on the scene. They wanted more than just your friendship. Sad for me because I enjoyed talking to males, but when I tried they would come with 'that' intention, so in the end I gave up.

At my school, currently we were leading a protest and going on strike due to a new part of uniform we didn't want. In Australia, we wear uniforms to school not casual clothing, and we didn't want the new uniform changes to be introduced, which in our mind were 'daggy black school shoes'. So 1,000 students went on strike, gathering together on our school oval, and a student had called the television news channel. It wasn't long before they arrived to get the news on the situation. They spoke to us as a group, and to a few individuals leading the strike to get our side of the story and why we were protesting, we never truly believed they would broadcast it, but that night we were all on the news Australia wide. It seems a little absurd now that such a small thing made headlines, but it was more about the way it happened. It happened because of a mass group of students that wanted to ban together, supporting each other, whilst revealing the passion driven by many of us to be heard. I'm not sure in the end if it was really about the shoes or more about students requiring some more respect in the education system, but nonetheless, we achieved a successful result. We won! New shoes were not introduced.

We had all come from the '70s, most of us born in the '60s. We had been raised in a generation of free speech, freedom of expression, the energy of the hippie revolution and the knowing of how important these qualities were conducive to living. We had grown up with more freedom, fun, laughter, less or little indoctrination, toxicity of technology, media, medication, and health issues in our world. We learned the power and importance of freedom without fear. That's not to say we still never became fearful or depressed, it was just a different time. We learned to stand up for what we believed in more so in those decades I believe than we do today. Kids weren't labeled like they are today and subjected to such

82

negative programming. In our time, we stood up for what we believed in. Our passion was a signature of who we were.

In saying that, a lot was about to change that brought extreme fear into this world. We were about to experience the global announcement of an epidemic that would sweep fear throughout this planet like no war ever had before. We were now also the first generation to experience the introduction of the ***AIDS epidemic*** which was to teach us that sex could kill you.

***

It was early '80s and a time we would all became terrified of sex, as it created an energy that if you had sex or used a needle, some people thought even if you kissed or held hands, we could get aids anytime, anywhere, from anyone!

Sex equaled death – and it became the most talked about topic. We couldn't escape it. Anyone that had unprotected sex thought they would end up with AIDS; the fear of catching AIDS spread quickly. It came upon us as what seemed overnight, and it rattled the world. It had been claiming lives previously; however, there was some trouble in identifying the disease. We were all pretty much in shock, and although, some of us where not sexually active yet (me included), we could see it wasn't going away anytime soon. This was a situation we would have to face when our time came. It was introduced and discussed in our schools and the AIDS crisis influenced every relationship. From that moment onwards, we became the generation of asking someone to get tested before we had sexual relations, as drastic as that sounded, it was real. This became a global fear, I remember very significantly the advertisements, news reports of people dying, and how devastating it was. People rejecting homosexuals, and it was plastered all around the world what this terrible disease was doing to humanity.

Teenagers were going through puberty, coming into themselves and sexuality. It was very much at the forefront of our minds. Whether you were already sexually active or not, it wasn't anything you could ignore, as it was our future… *And it was scary.*

Chapter 9
Outcast or Geek

Was I an outcast or geek, no idea, was there a difference? I kept people at an emotional arm's length, not just in school but everywhere, except for my family. They say people like us are different for a reason, and yes I'd heard all that before, but when you're growing up until you figure out why you're so 'different' for a 'reason', nothing flows easy when you're trying to be the same. At the time, we also don't realize being different, weird, strange, an outcast is actually a good thing. We just try to meander our way through life each day wondering what the next will bring, all the time (for me) wondering what I was here for. I know there are lots of kids out there that feel the same; we just remain loners, until maybe we don't. Maybe one day we will find that one person that understands us, *or maybe we never do.*

My sacred place was still home, and although, I was asked many times to have sleepovers with friends, I tried to decline nicely as much as I could, with a few exceptions. My friends were kind, caring, fun teenagers, and I liked them, but I just preferred my own company, that way I didn't have to layer masks. I didn't like groups, and I usually chose carefully who I wanted to spend time with, who got closer to me. I never 'let you in' very easily. Those early days of being judged and laughed at had crippled me, and I just couldn't let them go, or should I say the fear around that. I also wouldn't allow anyone to dishonor us and what we shared again. So I kept us protected and well hidden.

At times, I wondered if there was something wrong with me. My whole life so far I had been put down more than praised or paid compliments. I was always told that 'you're too tall', 'too lanky', 'your hips stick out', 'you talk too much', 'you're a nuisance', 'can you leave now?', 'what do you want?'. Often told I was blonde, (in other words dumb) laughed at for my ways. Sometimes, all I felt like was a nuisance. Instead of being said that I was too tall and lanky why couldn't I be told I was nice and slim, or how about just not mention that you can see my hips. I was ignored a lot by others which only enhanced my own feeling of being a nuisance. Because of this, I didn't feel good about myself at all really. When you constantly get told things like this, it does create wounds, wounds not easily healed, especially when you are so empathic. I could feel people's energy if they didn't want to be around me or thought I was becoming a nuisance. It's funny really, because the whole time I was trying to fit in I would have rather been quiet and on my own, then when I did try, I just spent my life being judged for it. *You kind of get judged either way. Did you notice that?*

Many hours were spent lying on my bed reading my bible (remember I'm not really referring to the bible, my bible was my *'Dolly'* magazine). I would await eagerly for its latest release and down to the shops I would walk to make my purchase. There were a few other magazines I purchased as well but *'Dolly'* remained my ever most efficient and up to date reliable source of latest trends, fashion, puberty issues, sex, music, and movie reviews. Also not forgetting the sealed Dolly doctor section, I would rip open the minute I secured the latest issue. Dolly doctor helped me with those delicate questions I was too embarrassed to ask, (the shy girl that would flush red as a beetroot and just want the ground to open up and swallow her) could not bring herself to ask a soul. So the sealed section became my 'survival'. *'Dolly'* had everything you needed to know and became a platform for our voices to be heard. Girls would write in to the Q & A section for advice which also showed me I wasn't the only loner out there. *'Dolly'* also provided us each edition with some much needed male 'hunky' pictures of the latest teen idols. Don't worry, they all had pants on, it was teen magazine.

***

As I sat in my English class at first period looking out the window, I was starting to feel even more pain than I had when I rose that morning. I headed off to school thinking it would subside, but instead, I became quite ill very quickly. The pain was unbearable. Immediately, I was taken from school to hospital to be examined and was rushed in for emergency surgery. I was quite violently ill by this stage and lying on a trolley in the corridor waiting to go through to theatre, I was a little nervous. I was 14 years old and wondering was this it, was this me over and out. Was I about to exit this weird world and be with my energy friend for good? As the doctor approached the bed to enlighten me on my condition, I braced myself.

"You have a ruptured appendix; it is serious that we operate immediately as complications could set in along with a risk of it being life threatening."

My Appendix had burst that morning and by 10:00 am I was in surgery. As anxious as I was due to the seriousness of my illness, I knew I was protected, I felt his energy around. With that wave of blissfulness, it appeared and I fully opened up to receiving, something inside me just trusted that I would be okay. (Not surprising that when I was half scared to death I had no choice to trust, and so I opened up to receive.)

Vulnerability was to play a key element in our energy exchange and soul connection. I needed my friend so desperately in this time, that connection and love would be what gets me through. I knew he would be with me in surgery, and as I was wheeled through those doors, peacefulness came over me. Although I didn't want to die, I also knew if I did he would be there waiting for me.

Waking up from surgery, I looked around and my first thought was, *yes, I am still here*. As much as I would have loved to see him, I was happy to stick around earth for a while.

The surgery went well but recovery was slower. I was awfully sick for several days, as I had an allergic reaction to the anesthetic. I wasn't particularly in a great way, but I felt calmness and peace around me. I felt I was being looked after, and by that I don't mean the hospital staff (not that they weren't). The feeling resembled a complete bubble of protection layered around me. It was in this moment that triggered just how incredibly protected I had felt my whole life.

There was a much bigger agenda going on here, one I had no idea about but I guessed one day I would find out.

I was hospitalized for a week, and although, it was a beautiful gesture that a few of my school friends came to visit me, I remember thinking, *oh, I wish they hadn't.* As appreciative as I was, at the time, I just wanted to be alone. I did not feel I was recovering as quick as I, perhaps, should have been. The allergy to the anesthetic had made me sick for days with being too weak to sit up and talk. I just needed and wanted to rest. Of course, my family came each day to visit, but I could be relatively myself with them.

A week later, I arrived home from hospital, and after a period of recovery, I returned to school and my life as normal.

Peer Pressure

The more I became lost in myself and the world around me, the more I sunk deeper into the world that can destroy you. A world that *we* humans have created for ourselves, despite there being a feeling of innocence it could still long destroy you if you let it. I became no different to anyone else really. Peer Pressure, wanting to fit in, not being bullied, or looked at strangely were all amongst the pressures we faced, me included. So I went looking for people that appeared to be covering up like me, so I could wear several masks and blend in. I found them. I had no idea why they wore their masks (like we all did), and I didn't ask. We all just knew each of us did for our own reasons. I could see they were, perhaps, more flawed than me; I hadn't had any particularly harmful earthly experiences at this point (apart from constant judgment) I was just trying to fit in. I was pretty sure no one would understand if I disclosed the real me with my attached energy friend along with the feeling of living between two worlds. It was a bit too far out for most people to comprehend, so I just left it at 'wanting a change'. Hopefully, they may accept me for whoever I pretend to be and not constantly make me feel I'm a nuisance. However, as I listened to them I could perceive they were doing it from a place of being hurt, abused, broken, damaged, and possibly like me, misunderstood in life from an earlier age. Whatever our reasons, it didn't matter, in some way we all chose to take the path of resistance. The path of natural flow would have served us better, but who knew about any of that.

It only took a few people to have judged me with my energy friend to catapult me into this life of 'covering up' the true essence of who I was, along with my ability to connect and bring forth my light – My light that I had brought into this world with me, my light which I had tried to disable from when I was seven years old.

So although I was doing well in school, I was struggling within. I decided to change my friendship group for this reason and the hope of some acceptance not judgment. In some slight way, perhaps, I wouldn't be judged so easily if I was with people who were the big shots in my year level. It may not have been the best decision for me in hindsight, but then, I needed to be accepted, not judged, and this may have been my ticket.

Again, being accepted by others does not define who we are. We all feel we need, have to have, acceptance from our friends, family, colleagues, but we do not. The only acceptance required is our OWN self-acceptance of who we are at our core, our soul. The big message here is to not let anyone else define you and stay true to yourself.

Putting on a front to be someone else was a way of protection. I had just broken up with my first boyfriend of six months. It was all quite innocent; he was a nice guy and quite the gentlemen. I had met him through a friend, and shortly after, we started dating. He didn't attend my school which worked well with my dating rule. (My one rule of dating was not to date anyone at my school – which I did stick to for my school days.) However, life was becoming increasingly more difficult for me due to my social anxiety.

The group I had gravitated to, they were known to be some of the 'toughest kids in school' and nobody messed with them. Why on earth did I gravitate to them, well I can't really be sure. For less judgment, to not be evaluated as often, maybe to reinvent myself with a whole new personality, or maybe it was just to rebel because I couldn't find my feet. One thing I did see, though, was that we were all lost in our own way. Whether you are a geek, nerd, tough, jock, weird, or popular; everyone is trying to find who they really are and where they fit in. Some just disguise it better than others, and some keep those masks on well into their life, forgetting who they really are.

A lie created to hide the truth eventually becomes the truth that we start to believe is real, whilst forgetting all along it is in fact the lie we created in the beginning. This is how one gets further and further disconnected from ones real authentic self. To this day, I really don't know what it was for me, but I was to spend the next year in a cycle of rebellious energy.

...and here's how that began.

I had never lied to my family, but I started too. I was rarely going where I said I was; and as my brother had left high school, by this time, he wasn't to see just who I was now associating with. I was free to do as I pleased. My grades started to decrease from As and Bs to Cs. I had become someone completely different and a person I didn't know. I ditched my current friends to hang around with the new ones, along with no explanation which was definitely not me. I adapted with masks to fit in perfectly. They never asked me why I had suddenly changed from this 'quiet, shy, smart, nerdy girl' to this tough, rebellious, try hard, but I think the head girl of our group had put it together. She never said a thing but I just knew she secretly understood me. I found someone in her that 'got me' without knowing the circumstances, so I gravitated to her friendship more. She was someone who wore a tough exterior; she projected to all around her that she did all the things we are 'not' supposed to do (even if she didn't do them), but she had this mystery to her. A mystery no one could really figure out. You could see it underneath, it was there, her incredible kind heart, gentle, and loving – a special soul but you had to look to discover it. Many took her at face value, which many do in life, and not many saw the hidden beauty or the mystery beneath. Perhaps, we both had more in common than even I recognized.

At home, I was still relatively the same, I had started to change a little but the mask I wore was only for school and outside interaction on weekends. I didn't change the music I listened too, TV shows I watched, or I didn't need to pretend with any of my interests, just how I acted I guess.

The saddest thing for me was immediately when I stepped into this role, my energy friend almost disappeared, I could hardly even feel him anymore. I think he had finally left me.

One school morning, unexpectedly, my new friend met me at the school gate I entered from for a quick chat. This wasn't usual; it wasn't like her to meet me there, but after our chat, I realized she didn't want me to be seen by teachers. She wanted us to skip school and the way I felt I didn't need any convincing. I had never ditched school before but it kind of sounded like fun. So we did.

In the '80s, we had what was known as 'Pinball parlors,' where pinball machines and all the arcade video games hung out in one spot for us to play. It became our local hang out. Skipping school to play these all day sounded more exciting than attending classes, so I said yes. This was a new side of me I hadn't yet seen. I rarely did anything wrong; I always stuck to the rules, but I started to think maybe that's my problem, sticking to the rules. I mean, perhaps, I needed to 'not stick to the rules so much'.

One day turned into two, which turned into three, four, and so on. For the first time in my life I felt like I fitted in, like someone accepted me and wanted to break the rules like me. I'd not felt confident to break the rules ever in my life to this point but always succumbed to 'the norm' as we know, hiding myself. I wasn't being my true self here either, far from it, but in a way it felt really good to go against society. I'd had enough of playing by the rules, and my new friend clearly felt the same.

I started drinking (what I thought was heavy alcohol) which turned out to be some cheap fruity wine, but it ticked the box for my new rebel self. My friend hung out with boys, which wasn't really my thing, but I started to as well. Before I knew it, I was surrounded by many along with a world of smoking, alcohol, and sex – my world had become remarkably different to anything I was used to. I was completely out of my comfort zone; I didn't engage in any of the activities (accept alcohol), but this was starting to become my new world.

Loading more masks numbing myself further beyond my soul.

We had fires on the beach at night, walked the streets everywhere and anywhere with no fear, and I lied about where I was. If my mother knew, she would have had a fit. I wasn't particularly enjoying my new life, yet in the old one I felt trapped within. I went with the notion that maybe breaking the rules and being more rebellious might help me to be more myself.

The lengths we go to keep running from ourselves. If only we knew to face our fears, which in hindsight are never as big as we see them. Our ego creates all these fearful thoughts and projected outcomes in our heads and we lose the courage to face them. Our mind constantly deceives us.

Acceptance in school is one of the biggest issues for youth, and for some reason, I didn't feel I was, although before my change, I did have friends, good grades, and was not bullied. I really wasn't the nerd or geek, nor popular, I was just cruising somewhere in between. I was starting to wonder if, perhaps, this was the better choice out of the two.

Our skipping school days turned into three weeks, what was I thinking? I wasn't at that time. It was pressure to be at school, perform, maybe have to expose myself and talk to the class so this seemed like a better option. But running away is never the better option. As we moved into higher levels of schooling it revealed even more class participation. Standing up or out in front of the class, reading passages, or worse, your essays, was terrifying for me, I just wanted to die. Anything that had all eyes on me and could potentially expose me to ridicule or laughter brought up too many childhood memories. This way, my new way, was much less stressful and kept my nervousness intact. There was no doubt I had a fear of public speaking, no prizes for guessing where that started, from a seven-year-old girl that was humiliated for speaking up. Prior to those events in my life, I never saw a time where being round others, exposing who I was, scared me. But I was just a little girl with no fear back then, being well guided and protected by my beautiful invisible friend.

We did get caught though, (as we foolishly wagged school every day consecutively) when one of my teachers phoned my mother to ask after me, with all these sick notes that were coming to school she was concerned. I became an expert at forging my mum's signature for the many days away, and it was all news to my mum, of course, as there was nothing wrong with me, she had been dropping me off for school on her way to work each morning. She was fairly shocked as this was not my normal behavior. So busted I was two weeks before I was to travel for my first overseas holiday. I was traveling to Fiji with some family members and Mum now wanted to stop me from going; however, it was too late to cancel my ticket so I expressed how extremely sorry I was, apologizing and promising I would not do it again. She allowed me to travel on the condition that things where to change when I returned. I did want to change my new ways, but I needed guidance as to how. I had created a messy situation.

I could feel him calling out to me, each time I stepped off my path, each time I acted from my free will and ego, not from us and my heart. I knew I was messing it all up, I knew I should have just been listening. I knew he was with me now to make a difference, a huge difference to bring that kind of awareness and openness to others, but I was too fearful of others disrespecting what we had. At the same time, I knew in my heart what we had was rare and needed to be shared.

Well, there was no more skipping school, I wouldn't do that again, aside from the fact it was senseless I didn't really enjoy it. Well, I did the first few days, but then it became boring, and I now had to catch up on all my class work I'd missed. Wasn't exactly my smartest decision but in some way it felt good, although, this time I had sunken deeper into 'who knows what'. I still proceeded to hang around with the same people, but I decided to attend school each day. We really weren't doing anything that bad. I wasn't exactly the badass I thought I was, not rebel material at all. As much as I tried it just wasn't me.

Sometimes, at school and in life, we look for ways to fit in or make our life easier. We pretend to be cool, smart, tough, strong, funny, many things whilst selling ourselves short. We are rejecting our very own core perfect self, our beautiful soul, and the true being we are. God/The universe/Divine, whatever you chose to call it all made us different, we are not all the same, because life would be very boring and quite robotic if we were all made the same. We are all different for a reason and that's what makes life so interesting. What one does another wouldn't, what one likes, another doesn't. We are here to choose our own path and that path of which we have come to earth for. You are not here to live the same path as your best friends, your parents, your siblings, your friends, anybody else's. You're here to live yours; plain and simple, and we can do that whilst interacting with others, but it's so imperative that we stay on our own path not theirs. This is why validation and acceptance from others is not necessary, and their opinions should definitely not shift you off your own course. When we want other's acceptance, it again falls upon what they would do or how they would live, and that would be following *their* choices – not *yours*.

***

As I flew out to Fiji for my first overseas holiday, I was happy to escape my world for a while. Two weeks of fun in the sun sounded exciting, five of us altogether, my aunt was lovely enough to take us – my brother, myself, and our two older male cousins. It was our first trip for all of us; my aunt never had a family of her own as yet and looked to her sisters children as hers too. She wanted to take us overseas to explore new cultures and have the experience of an extended view of life, and we were very grateful. It was to be relaxing and peaceful, so I was looking forward to it, plus being around family I could be somewhat more myself.

Experiencing a new culture, watching their lifestyle, and how they lived was another eye opener for me. The island was so laid back, everyone taking their time, no rushing or anger, and the energy was beautiful. It projected energy of a peaceful paradise. To be surrounded by palm trees and lush gardens, traditional Fijian food, and their extreme generosity was exceptionally enjoyable. I was loving it!

We had been on the island three days soaking up the sun, swimming, relaxing in such a tranquil setting by the pool when we girls decided to have a day out shopping. We had discovered there was not a lot of shopping to do in Fiji, but we could explore what they had on offer visiting the local tourist shops and markets picking up some souvenirs, plus almost getting arrested!… It was to be a complete misunderstanding that went something like this.

After making our purchases for the day, we returned to the resort only to be called upon quickly to reception. Standing over us in the foyer was a Fijian police officer all decked out in his traditional uniform looking about 8 feet tall (which might be a slight exaggeration). As he spoke, fear ran through my body and the hair on my arms stood up. He was so very intimidating. His half smile over his extreme authority voice and frown was confusing. We were clueless as to why he was there or what he wanted with us; we hadn't broken the law. As he started to speak, the moment felt surreal and I immediately found myself thinking, *where are you, please protect me, please help me, are you there?* I was referring to **him**, my beautiful love. Again, in this position being faced with a very live physical situation I wasn't sure how much he could do because he wasn't in physical presence, but I was hoping he could wave some type of magic to clear it all up. Oh, god, please. Where was he! As the fear of life was running through me, my ego was having a field day with that little voice, telling me, "Oh, that's right. He has disappeared; he got sick of you trying to become all sorts of **fake** versions of yourself. He's had enough of you letting him down; he's gone now, never to return." I couldn't blame him if he had, I had not been so nice to him/us, and I'd not felt him for a while now.

The Police officer started questioning us about our whereabouts, times, what we had purchased in the shops, and he wanted to take our passports so we couldn't leave the country. My fear levels were now in overdrive. As he was asking more questions, I suddenly felt a wave of peace enter my body, and I just knew we would be okay. I knew I was being looked after, and all would be fine. He proceeded to say that two white girls had stolen from the shop we browsed in earlier that day, but when we explained how long we had been in Fiji he knew it wasn't us. These girls had been stealing for some time, long before we arrived, and the police had been attempting to catch them. We also didn't fit the description or nationality of two offenders in their early twenties, so he let us go. This was not the ideal experience you wanted in a foreign country at 15 years of age, not to mention my first overseas trip. I wondered if the universe was at play. Would they really attempt to scare me half to death to re-connect with my energy friend, to come back to myself, my roots? If it was they played it well, because that's exactly what I did, in addition I saw him once again in action and how so beautifully I'm protected. Perhaps, he was trying to give me a wakeup call to shift me back onto my true path. I couldn't blame him for being cross with me or using this situation to get my attention. I deserved it. *But maybe he wanted me back after all.*

After our ordeal that day, we tried not to let it dampen our holiday spirits, and so we returned to the relaxing surrounds for the remainder of the trip and chalked it up to another vacation experience, one we would be happy not to relive.

After two weeks, our relaxing trip had come to an end, and it was time to depart. We had all enjoyed a wonderful time amidst sarongs, palm trees, and coconuts, sunbathing and relaxing by the pool and soaking up the authentic Fijian culture. I truly did love its beauty and surrounds, not to mention its peacefulness and serenity 'go slow' atmosphere.

As I traveled back on the plane from Fiji into Melbourne, I knew somehow things had to change. I needed to blend my reality of my life with the reality of who I really was, but how was I to do that?

As I lost myself deeper and deeper into my new identity, you might ask where my energy friend was, weren't they always walking with me? Guiding me?

Well, I was feeling my energy friend less and less. But that wasn't because of him, it was me. The further I distanced myself from my soul, my heart, my love, the more I chose to live and create my reality from my fears – not from love. The less I could be guided or helped. The less I paid attention.

I had now become this person where all traces of my light had vanished.

***

From those young childhood days of being able to see, feel, and hear. Then to later feeling and hearing, now it seemed I could only feel, and that was becoming rarer. I now felt well-embedded into this world and had shut out anything of a higher consciousness. At this point, I didn't even talk about angels or anything metaphysical, nor admit I even believed in them. I still prayed to god each night (or to the higher presence) before I closed my eyes to sleep, this was a not negotiable for me no matter who I was pretending to be that week. Peer pressure had now taught me to live from outside of myself as opposed to spirituality where we live from the inside out. There was no doubt I was awaken to the spiritual world and a conscious way of living since I was born, but I never met anyone who talked about spirituality, psychics, being intuitive, feeling energies, natural healers, or anything of that nature. (Where were all these people – I knew they were out there somewhere.)

When we studied in school about native traditional cultures and how they lived from the land, especially Native American Indians, I was mesmerized, completely drawn in to listen feeling much resonated with me, it was a little bizarre. As I flicked through books, seeing pictures of this time, and how they lived (and in some cases still do), I would get visions flashing before me, visions I had not seen before or that weren't in the books, but visions like I had experienced these before. It drew me in like I had lived this life, like I had been one myself and the familiarity felt intense. I always believed in past lives, that was a given because I knew I was an old soul. I guessed somewhere in those past lives I had spent within these cultures.

I was to learn decades later by a few world renowned healers and from my soul records that I was in fact an incredible medicine woman/shaman over thousands of lifetimes on earth with my soul partner, along with many other master abilities – I wasn't here this time, in this life, to do that again, but I could easily tap into those gifts if I wished

97

– and often I do. This would make sense to me why I resonated so well and felt it so intense in those earlier years.

One soul, joined by two entities, bonded together from two worlds. A combined energy force directing me through a powerful presence, where I felt it maneuver through me and out like a floating energy of pure love flowing within. The feeling of being caught in a physical and non-physical reality. One energy but the presence of two traveling this road of life, directing us safely with the pure unconditional love and life force, but yet I couldn't get out of my own way to just allow, receive, be shown. Whatever it was I knew I carried with me; it wasn't a connection because it was part of me so not making a connection to a separate part. This much I had worked out. What it meant I had no idea. When I felt it fully, the missing piece faded, when I couldn't feel it, my void returned. I suppose the only other way to possibly describe the sensation was another one of me but not in human form, an extension of myself, identical in energy; soul, knowing, but I just couldn't see this other half.

We all have free will to a point and our ego can direct our free will choices away from where we are meant to be. Fear of acceptance for being different. They knew and would have guided silently, but I panicked. I thought I couldn't do this, and my fear took over.

Feeling this energy with me through my life made me feel extremely blessed; I knew without it I would have been more lost. It traveled with me to keep me on track, and although, my free will did at times run off course, imagine if I never had it. This incredible love energy friend washed over me so ecstatically that it always bought me back to my soul, reminding me who I really was, the real me, showing me my true essence, my light, and for that I was so very grateful.

I was the luckiest person in the world to have such an experience. I think the key was to graciously allow the direction of the flow it was sending me towards, instead of fighting it with my fear of not fitting in or being judged. Originally I was open to the complete experience, until I wasn't. A child grows up, matures, and feels peer pressure to fit in all ways. I was not blaming myself, but I had made a bit of a mess of things overall. Trying too hard may have just been the problem, going with the flow was always best. Not that we always know this when younger, or older in some cases, as a lot of humans rather control than go with the flow. I must say though he never gave up on me, he always walked with me, even when I couldn't feel him present.

I never really comprehended in my youth that this energy was actually joined with me, so it couldn't leave. I was the one causing the feeling like it came then left, through being disconnected from myself, my soul. Like I said earlier, when we are connected to our heart and soul we feel our true essence, we are our true self, so obviously I was going to always feel him present. When I disconnected, layered masks, and took on alternative egos, live entirely within the matrix materialistic world, of course I'm not as connected, so he will fade. Switching to live from ego disconnects us, ironically one does not realize and often in some cases never realizes. How many, I wondered, grew up remaining their true self, and how many didn't – but made it back there. How many live from feeling and not thinking? How many resist instead of surrendering? And how many don't even recognize this is apparent and vital to formatting their whole life, living from heart and soul, love, peace, and flowing abundance. Until this side of oneself is untapped, you can't possibly live an authentic life, and *most will usually create a living, not a life.*

***

Fleetwood Mac was my choice when I was always chillin' out on my bed with 'my bible'. Stevie Nicks had a way of filling any room with a laid back mood. I loved her down to earth relaxed style and hippie energy. Even at her concerts, she showed this same hippie type essence on stage. Every time she came to Australia, I made sure I was at her concerts, I loved her!

The disco scene had almost left us, its days were numbered (bye, bye, disco). It was a little sad, though, because it brought a funky happy upbeat vibration that rippled throughout. I could see the world of music was now changing, bringing with it a much lower vibrational feel. Despite this, the music scene was creating powerful content where some artists were using lyrics to escape and express their points of view across to the collective. This was helping us unite more as one, which was well needed.

Johnny Depp and Tom Cruise were my teen idols. Bruce Springsteen. 'The Boss' was fast becoming another favorite and dance movies were hitting the screen which brought me much happiness.

At school, we were still writing notes in class, turning them into paper airplanes to fly them across the room to friends. I didn't really participate much, as I didn't have many friends or knew how to make a successful paper airplane that flew past my chair. If it wasn't flying quick and snappy, we were 'sprung' and mine were never snappy so I often remained more a spectator. It was a lot of fun watching people get caught

The Joys of the '80s Before Technology

Swimming at the ocean beach was a regular gig when the sun was shining, and I was so lucky it was only ten minutes away. When I wasn't going for recreation, I would still travel down with my father, and we would scour the sand for cuttlebone for his birds all year around. Whilst there, I would collect shells for myself and dip my feet in the water, feel the cleansing of my body from the salt water. I loved the smell of the ocean, the sound of the waves, and the magic of not being able to see where the water stopped and the sky began. As the sun set on the ocean waves, I would look in amazement and always wish I had remembered to bring my camera. I discovered I'm a soul that is so connected to the ocean that I couldn't imagine ever living far away from it. Watching the surfies did not go amiss either, hotties on the water. I loved surfies, their free spirited nature, but watching from the sand was enough, riding a board was not something I tried until a few years later. I always thought for sure that I would date or end up with a surfie. Why? I have no idea, but perhaps, I could feel their free spirit, their soul souring free from the earthly constraints around us, and perhaps, I even thought they might understand me more than others.

For the first time in my life, it didn't feel bad to be known, but the girl I had become was not the girl I was inside. I'd created a whole new identity and through her I could express, release, and become a stronger powerful person. I was inevitably filling my void I had felt my whole life with this new character (alter ego) and in a way it felt good. As we come to learn, though, void fillers have an expiration date, and mine was coming to her end.

I had played out this alter ego character for almost a year now, playing the same game. However, playing two different people – one outside of my home and another inside was starting to become increasingly difficult. It was also making me just feel empty inside. My heart was pushing up against the person I really was, and as I started to feel more lost in my new world, I became even more lost overall. How long could I keep it up for? Would I stay in the world that was definitely not me as a rebellious person but it seemed a little more fun hiding, or would I let go of my new personality and go back to the real me. Although I didn't really know who 'she' was anymore, well I did, but I just never seemed to be able to shake that fear.

The missing piece or void I was always searching for was becoming painful and harder to live without. At this point, I wasn't sure if continuing on my rebellious way would find my missing piece, or maybe it was only something I could find when I was being more my authentic self. I was sick of being the Kellie at school, another Kellie with friends, and another at home. When I sat back and looked, I was a different Kellie depending on where I was or who I was in the company of. Too many different Kellies but none were the real one, my true self.

As the weeks passed, a series of events and actions occurred that were very unpleasant and forced me to really close up. I wasn't sure what to do but I knew I had to change my life again. This, whatever I was doing was clearly not working for me, and I felt once again the universe was showing me – as harsh as it needed to be – '*that we will make the decision for you*', or at least someone was. Due to this, I left 'her' behind in a very quick transition that basically happened overnight and returned to the 'more' authentic me. I still wasn't functional as the real me but let's just say I was a few steps closer.

Why was I trying so hard to fit in, when I was here to stand out?

Chapter 10
Too Many Identities

What does that mean exactly? How can we have too many identities? Well when you look at it often we all do, we just don't realize. We take on a different character for our current circumstance. No different to being in the movies really. One for work, one for school, one for family, one for friends, maybe even one for your partner because let's face it how many partners really do see the true you? Perhaps, sometimes we don't even know how to be ourselves. Maybe your light might scare you, or much worse you're dark. Perhaps, most don't even realize any of this and just plod along getting through each day in their life hoping for a 'good day' but not understanding why life is this way. Why there are ups and downs. Yet again, everyone has been told by their parents and those around them growing up that life will always be this way, so that little program recorded into their subconscious mind remains and plays out over and over their entire life. They are constantly hitting the replay button when necessary, when that embedded related thought or feeling arises, and we react accordingly. Most don't even realize we can, in fact, hit the stop button and reset. We can re-program our subconscious thoughts and fears.

My theory with the identities: how often do we really want to open ourselves up to who we really are? We shut down, we are in fear of getting hurt, heartbroken, laughed at, judged, bullied, hated (because let's not forget the haters – they are coming from their own place of pain).

Often in life, if you have something others want or you are in a happy personal place where they aren't, they will be envious; they often won't want *you* to have it either. We become mirrors, and those trigger in another *their* very own fears and insecurities.

But with 'identities', why do we find it extremely hard to show ourselves in every way, exactly who we are at a soul level? Why don't we feel comfortable shining our light? Why don't we feel comfortable loving ourselves, sharing our love, opening to that love, being honest, truthful, completely opening deeply to being our true authentic selves? Because living from this place brings us a life full of love, happiness, abundance and peace, inside and out, so why would we ever choose anything else? It makes no sense does it? Just like living in fear makes no sense. Following along with everyone else on their social beliefs and structures like sheep, makes no sense. Not being accepted for who you are, being judged by society, and let's face it the list could go on for a very long time, but you can see when it's observed this way it all makes no sense to live from anything else but our *TRUE AUTHENTIC SELF.*

When we really sit back and look at life, this existence we have 'created' for ourselves it looks insane. Just take yourself out of the 'Matric box' for a moment and go into your heart. You will clearly see exactly how insane, ridiculous, and strange it all is. Nothing makes sense about the way we all live; everything is driven by fear and rarely driven from love. Yet if we were to flip that and all live from a place of love – not fear – the standard of life we create for ourselves is astoundingly different and flourishing. Being your true self for a start, because you won't fear what anyone thinks is the number one key. People worrying about what others think of them, I call this the number one 'disease' of our world. Fearing judgment, rejection, acceptance, or wanting validation, all create our insecurities. In return, this creates the domino effect of people being 'afraid' to live from their true self. When we live a life from our heart and soul, our authentic self, we live a life from a place of greater consciousness which results in peace, abundance, bliss, being compassionate, sharing kindness and caring, shining our light. We also become aware of the importance of health and wellbeing using the most advanced natural healing techniques, learning to understand energy – *because everything IS energy* – and all that is, being guided by our intuition. But all of this is called – weird, crazy, scary, insane, and airy fairy way out stuff! Can you believe that? When you look at the two ways of living in this world – Oh, yes – I could see how this would be enough to frighten everyone half to death. Now, do you see how stupid that sounds?

Awakening is not some 'rocket science degree' that we need to be able to wake up and see the world around us for what it is. Even for the most stubborn person, they would have to be blind to not see it, but as long as we have fear, ignorance, and resistance attached, people will not see a way for a better life.

I was resisting being my true self, for fear of judgment and was ignorant to the fact that life would never go well for me until I stopped resisting. We have some great days. Maybe even a good year now and then, but life never flows when we live from lower vibrational (fear based) energies and emotions. It's just not possible! 'So my many identities' – I had created through my 'resistance' of truly being who I was, and to shine my light accordingly, whilst not being too afraid of others people's reactions. Even those that say, "I don't care what others think" will in some way manipulate their thinking to avoid being exposed to the fears they have secretly embedded within them, often not even knowing they are there. People then wonder why they don't have amazing, abundant filled, sensational, joyful, peaceful, loving, incredible lives and relationships. Because when you don't know how to get from okay to amazing, or from 'just settling to sensationally fulfilling in every way', we just keep plodding and settling. Hoping, wishing, life will improve and being envious of those that have this.

So it was beneficial that I realized there were way too many Kellies to choose from, and I had to find my way back to me. This may be my first part to taking the path of non-resistance. I had a 'non-resistant awareness' happening for the first time in my life. But now *who* was I really, I mean I knew who I was behind the mask, but how do I get back there and 'remain there'.

Life just felt like it had thrown me another curveball.

When we keep layering fake parts of ourselves over and over through life, how difficult is it to actually find your way back to you? In my case – 'Very'.

Remember what they say about 'old souls' we don't mix all that well or fit the 'mold' so for us, when you know all your life who you really are but are ignoring that part of you inside, who you are as a soul, it eats away at you. It eats away until you step up and claim it. Owning who you are and what you're here for, and until you do, you might find the universe will ride your backside until you do.

Own it. Claim it, step into it and create from this incredible love which is, *'Your Soul'*

Somewhere deep inside, she was there, crying out, screaming even, like a child being trapped in a cage, but after many years, *'had I locked the door and thrown away the key?'* When you're judged early in life for being different, and you realize you 'can't' be who you really are in a world where 'you think' fitting in is of the highest priority, it does pose the question *how do we get back there.*

Often our ego has a little chat with us about fitting in, and it goes a little like this:

EGO: "You have to fit in no matter what the consequences- End of story!" (Not much of a chat! But it's recorded and on reply).

Living this way was no longer an option – so where would I start. Returning to that little girl, the one that didn't have any fear, that's where I would start, that's where I would find myself again. I could also connect and ask my energy friend to guide me which sounded even better! (And this time, I would listen.) All I had to do was open my heart, connect within to my soul completely and he would be here, I could hear him. But where would I find the courage to then show others who I was, who I traveled with and what I could feel? I was back to the same situation of wondering if people would understand or accept me. That could potentially mean opening myself up to being ostracized just like when I was little, when I was being myself. Even if I didn't care, what would I tell people? Would the conversation go something like this?

"Surprise, I hadn't told anyone because I was keeping it a secret, but I am actually an old soul and completely someone different. I talk to cover up my true self, I don't like being around many people, and I have metaphysical abilities. I've actually walked all my life with a connected energy that I'm bonded with, and that shows me love like no love on this planet, plus I feel like I'm torn between two worlds."

My ego replies: "Yep, I'm sure that would go down really well, and I wouldn't get bullied or called nuts at all. Right then let's do this... NOT.

My heart and soul speaks: "I need to stop resisting and release that fear of judgment I've lived with my whole life. Who cares what others think and if they thought I was weird or don't fit in, what exactly do I want to fit in to? Their life sure wasn't great; I would choose my experience over theirs any day, so why was this so difficult?"

After much thought, my ego got the better of me. All I kept seeing was how difficult it would be because I was a teenager in a high school. I would be choosing to return to the painfully shy, different, and introverted girl, and feel like an outcast. But I decided this I would do, and gradually I may be able to be my true self.

Covering up had become a chore, how do people do this all their life. It's exhausting, (although I was very good at it) but feeling increasingly more lost, alone, and confused. I was back to being an introvert for now, which wasn't ideal but was more me.

***

Being back to my introverted self, I had forgotten, had its downfalls. To sit in a class room and learn was not difficult for me if the teacher just ignored me, but often this wasn't the case. I started to see some teachers just simply had the urge to humiliate and embarrass you in front of others, why? I had no idea. They especially seemed to hone in on the shy kids. Well, that's the energy I felt, and it was my experience. If my teachers were having a bad day, I could rest assured I was about to as well? Was it the thrill of being disrespectful and calling me out by my surname – I could never figure out in school why they did this – or the horrific look on my face when they did? There is always that one teacher that is a pain in the ass, treating you like you're his prized tool for the day whilst he's being the only tool in the classroom. I do refer to a male as this was my situation, but I'm not ruling out a feminine authority figure getting her kicks just the same. It was sheer embarrassing, and it became a regular occurrence. At some point, though, I found my voice in their classes and yes, surprisingly, I did speak up. My Aries fire would spark with intense displeasure, and I started to stick up for myself, 'as shaking in my boots as I was', it did feel good, until I got kicked out of class. But I did have courageous moments, and I chalked that up to progress. (Even if I was sitting outside the classroom with a smile on my face – badass revisited!)

I had changed back over night and walked away from the alter ego naughty girl, with no explanation. Keeping the reasons to myself, I never shared. Reasons I could not spend time with my group anymore, events that occurred outside of school that changed everything, but I kept them to myself. I wasn't into explanations; I rarely shared any personal details about myself, (as we know) even to the closest of friends. I was not a sharer. I kept everything private to prevent being gossiped about or spread around (because girls can't help themselves sometimes) in the event, it became an embarrassing situation.

Adolescent years can be exciting but tricky at the same time. We are maturing, discovering, trying to find our feet in many different ways. I had kept contact with my past boyfriend, the one I had left in hast to find more excitement and be the rebel. He wanted me back, and I wanted to come back, so I did. I adored him in many ways. He was kind, caring, easy going, and extremely different to other boys I had met in my past year. I was never really attracted to the 'Bad Boy' type, or the resilient, tough, macho types of guys, I'm not sure why but they just didn't interest me. I liked more authentic, quiet, carefree-natured guys, ones that didn't need to bring attention to themselves, ones that felt they had nothing to prove.

Up until now, I had not connected with or found anyone that made me feel that love from my energy friend. They were early days, and I was still only a teenager but when you start to become attracted to another or others, you begin to develop an understanding of different connections, energies, loves. By this stage, I had experienced a few boyfriends and been aware of my feelings with them all. Nothing, no other experience or feeling had come anywhere remotely close to what I had felt so far, and a feeling deep down inside of me knew it probably never would.

Chapter 11
Beaches

It was summer of '82 and in Australia, at these times, we had long hot summers over Christmas and beyond whilst majority of the world were having winter. Having an older sibling of four years, certainly, pushed the boundaries of growing up fast, and perhaps, viewing things earlier than one normally would. Anyone with older siblings, I'm sure can relate. We become exposed to mature things earlier, earlier than our eyes would glimpse and our minds might understand them. For me, I already felt old (as we well and truly have established – again!) and mature was my middle name (unfortunately), so I had gone from *'Ice Castles'* to *'Summer Lovers'* in four short years, but those movies were worlds apart.

'Ice Castles' was my favorite movie for a long time, and I had its theme song *'Looking through the eyes of love'* on replay for years as a young girl. The lyrics talked to me ever so profoundly. It was exactly how I felt with him, my heart would open so deep, and it spoke to my soul. I was hiding what I feared would be taken from me. Each time I didn't want the feeling to end because I feared it might not come again. My heart was wide open to him, and I could feel all the love he brought forth with us, 'Reaching out to touch you' and feeling so much love, it was talking to me in every way. I got lost in those lyrics, they constantly brought me back to *me – my soul – us* and for a girl so young I understood so well.

'Summer Lovers' took me to a different place with a passion for life and a burning desire to keep searching – *'The beautiful Santorini – Greek islands'* burst onto the screen and it took my breath away. Travel was something I always intended to do some day, but I'd not given it much thought until now, I was pretty much a home body. However, after watching that

movie I was hooked, hooked on travel, Santorini, the Greek islands and exploring. Not so much the exploration of threesomes that were portrayed in the movie, but the adventures, freedom, open nudity that was accepted. Not being afraid to explore and be yourself, who I was truly yet to be, but watching it portrayed on screen gave me hope I could one day do the same. Shy I was, but underneath I did have a yearning to express and experience new things. It cracked open that part of me that craved to free my soul and to find the courage within to execute such a thing. It was a movie of growth between three people where they faced their fears within unexpected situations. By releasing their fears as they arose, they opened the doors to discover even more fun, love and laughter, growth, and trust amongst all. They discovered an unconditional love within their relationships as opposed to a conditional love controlled by their fear. The movie comprised of many deeper messages if you took notice – *which I did* – and struck me as quite an open conscious movie.

We learn to discover, grow, and shape ourselves through an array of different teachings, readings, viewings, some more influential than others. For me, it was about what I truly connected with, despite how that information or insight came to me. I think current events or situations, movies, music, media, all influence us, but we take on board what most resonates with our true self, our heart. We take on what feels right and leave the rest. Whether those things are truly right for us or not we don't know, but they mold us into the people we are today and the persona we project. We enter this world with a soul and heart but our personalities are made up as we go. You will always be the child inside but depending on how well you live from that truth, or how well you layer with masks will depend on how your personality shapes you. To me, personalities can be false. I could tell you hundreds of people that believe my personality is the real me, but it's not. I'm manipulating my personality (or the one people see) to suit my needs, fears, people's possible judgments, because that's the one I want people to see, but it is not the real me.

Summer days, when you're a teenager, are usually spent having fun, socializing, beaching and pretty much doing as little work as possible – my summers were no different, with the exception maybe of not socializing a great deal. We frequented the ocean beach with friends or family, depending on the day, and it was the trend to go topless sunbathing – well I did say it was the '80s – however, not something we did when beaching with our family, girlfriends yes. Although Europe was a hot spot for full nudity on some beaches, it hadn't quite caught on in Australia, so it was just the ladies doing the nudity not the guys (unfortunately).

This summer, I decided it would be fun to take surfing lessons, I'm not sure what I was thinking but *'Summer Lovers'* had inspired me to try all sorts of new experiences. My cousin surfed, and as he was staying with us over the holidays, he graciously offered up his time to teach me. So here I was on the board, on my knees attempting to stand up, and I did pretty well under the circumstances, but my attempts were short lived when it dawned on me there were sharks living in these waters as well. Sharks terrify me. So as much as I tried to keep my cool, I knew my fear of deep water and sharks combined, possibly wouldn't bring a positive outcome. As I considered my situation some more while I was watching those waves further out, the ones I would have to paddle out to actually surf on, I decided surfing wasn't such a great idea after all, and so back on the sand I went. With that, my surfing days were over pretty much before they began. But I did get up on my knees, so I ticked the box for that one.

I feel, perhaps, my fear of sharks had originated back when I was ten years old. Our family were out fishing in our boat one day when we had a slight altercation with an extremely large Hammerhead shark. Well it felt like an altercation to me. We were closer to shore in more shallow waters cleaning the fish we had caught that day, and the water was crystal clear. The shark swam alongside our boat brushing itself up against it whilst circling the boat. Our boat was 18 feet long, and this shark looked almost as big; it even gave my dad a fright. At the time, he swiftly kicked the engine over hoping the shark would move on, which it did, however, we then watched it head towards a skier on the water. We watched as they were heading towards each other, hoping and praying the skier wouldn't see the shark, or he would probably fall out of fear. It could have gone either way and we held our breath, but luckily as we watched the skier skied right over the top of the shark. He continued on, we could breathe again. Its fin was out of the water, so I'm sure the skier would have noticed, but if he did, he chose not to panic, which saved his life. It all happened so quickly but it's a memory I have most vividly, and I have no doubt this is the reason I'm discouraged from entering into deep waters.

I was quite proud of myself years later, though, when I faced my fears a little and took up bodyboarding instead. I know it wasn't surfing, and I still to this day wish I could surf but, I'm happy and content with bodyboarding

So back on the sand wasn't all that bad anyway, perving on the surfies whilst being out of the water was much more relaxing than being in. Sun, sand, and surf, we loved our beach days! It wasn't jumping of the cliffs of Santorini but we felt blessed to have this at our backdoor. (Are there sharks in Santorini – hmm I wonder)

Our summer nights were warm well into the evening, and we would sometimes swim in pools or the shallow front beach till midnight. We spent more beautiful days and nights outdoors with nature (as modern technology had not been introduced), using our own guidance and intuition to explore, adventure, and find exciting things to do. We went bushwalking in the valley, cliff walking to the lighthouse, picnics in the park, horseback riding along the beach, scenic coastal walks. We explored secret beach coves with warm rock pools to lounge in, secluded from the outside world feeling free to be naked. (Until someone else found them too) It didn't matter, we had plenty of choices and felt free to explore. Being around nature gives you an incredible feel for energy along with our planets majestic beauty, it's like you can see the energy vibrating off the plants and trees, and the purity as you breathe in the fresh air. There were an abundance of opportunities close to home for a small coastal peninsula if we opened our eyes. We lived in a beautiful place, but some people were blinded to our hidden gems, because they simply didn't venture out and discover.

I wonder how many explore like this today or are most too busy with cell phones glued to their hands, X-boxes, internet, TV, and social media.

We were the last generation that experienced Mother Nature and all its glory without the inclusion and indoctrination of all modern devices that take us away from our heart and soul activities. I feel so truly blessed I grew up in a time before the world became a far different place.

Even the movies were much lighter in these times, although it did appear that horror films were now on the rise after a few box office successes. I watched my first horror film around this time, which was not really by choice. I screamed, jumped, and had an all-round horrible, frightening, intense, nerve-wracking experience. I decided I would never put myself through that again, although I may have watched a few more under 'complete peer pressure' from friends and hated every moment of it. The things we do to fit in! I never understood why society made films like this. It was such high impact drama to be spreading out to the world.

Teen movies were on the rise as well in different ways, they were funny, heartfelt, showing love, making a point. Looking between the lines many were educational for us, but we may not have fully comprehended that at the time. Some were telling deeper stories, but it depended on where your mindset was at, as to what journey you took beyond the surface.

Throughout the summer, our beloved music got a good workout as well. We played music every day, took it to the beach with us, on walks, picnics, wherever we went, listening to whatever complimented my mood on that day. Michael Jackson was becoming another incredible awakened artist that was showing us through his music. He had released his latest album *'Thriller'* that year which would go down in history as being one of the greatest albums of all time. An eccentric performer that had a message; he knew who he was and what he was here for. His unique expression and flavor as an artist in addition to his soft gentle nature was to serve a greater purpose for our world. You could feel he had been sent to earth at this time as one of the greats to help humanity. His lyrics and music were to make such an impact on the world. There will never be another Michael Jackson!

Fun and uplifting music, dancing, movies, the drive-in, beaches, outdoor activities, peace, connection, and nature was my jam (plus I loved board games – especially monopoly) but anything else felt like drama to me. Being outdoors cleared the mind, adventure created excitement, peace helped us to connect, and fun activities made us laugh, keeping it simple!

Until life got difficult.

Chapter 12
Transition

Summer holidays had now finished and life was back to 'not so much fun'. I was 16 and in my Fourth year of high school. As I stepped back on campus, I felt more alone than ever. School was the last place I wanted to be.

Feeling him all summer was different to the usual way I felt him with me. We had transitioned, and I was now feeling like he was inside me, almost like he had jumped inside me, and it felt very different than before. Maybe we had integrated further into one another, I can't really be sure how to explain it, but I just knew it felt like he was not connected to me or walking next to me, but in me. He never spoke to me anymore, or that I heard, but his energy was just there. Silence seemed to be the way now.

Those days of sitting on my bed talking to him, risking someone walking in thinking I was crazy talking to fresh air, I still tried. I had continued to talk to him well into my teenage years; it was just him and I. But now when I talked to him, I received nothing in return. Even those days when I thought I was connecting so deeply within my soul, myself, there was nothing. No words, no guidance, nothing. Something had changed, and he didn't want to talk anymore. We became this energy that just didn't communicate, yet I could still feel him. I started to wonder, now that I was mature was it time for him to leave. Was this why he was quiet? I suppose I was at an age where he thought I could now do this myself; perhaps, because I had a boyfriend (did that bother him?). I would think not given where his spirit was residing – from the place of unconditional euphoric love. Did he feel though I had betrayed him? But he wasn't in my world present for me to be with him. So I'm sure he would understand. Physically, I was well mature now, and at times, I did wonder just how much he 'sees of me' (my embarrassing shyness), then I saw how absolutely ridiculous my thoughts were, because we are all naked in the other world, they can see anything. Why should this worry me anyway? He was part of me. He knew me better than I knew myself. I wondered, *does he want to be here with me. Does he wish he was physically walking with me so we can be together?* I had many questions because our communication had changed, and I wasn't receiving anything back, it felt like he was slipping away.

As my heart softened, I imagined that. Imagined if he was real in this physical world how incredible our life would be, and how much love we would share, however, in all my attempts when younger to pull him into my reality or ask him, he never came. I longed to be with him, to see him, to see what he would really look like, but was he now leaving me. He had left an imprint all over my heart and soul, an imprint that would remain forever. And I'm not sure what I would do if he left. Despite the wonder, I never gave up; I still hoped for that one day and always believed that day would come.

A lot of youth around the world suffer bullying in school, and it looked like I was no exception. At a time when I was trying to figure out myself, catch up on my schooling, and explore career choices to discover exactly what I wanted to do with my life, a few people decided it would be interesting to mess with me. I wasn't with the 'in group' anymore and had no protection.

Part of me felt like 'do what you want to me'. I was feeling the void more than ever since he felt so distant, and I couldn't really care less about anything else. I just wanted him back, talking to me, guiding me.

Being tall was an advantage for if I had to fight, but if I turned sideways you could hardly see me, that's how slim I was. With not a lot of weight on me, I contemplated would I want to tackle more than one, did I want to tackle any? Not really, not at all, but I had always stuck up for myself and this would be no exception. I hated confrontation and drama, remember, and I would go out of my way to avoid them, but sometimes you just can't avoid the school bullies. I was not scared of them; I just didn't want the attention or distraction to my studies. I planned on returning and laying low, flying way under the radar with my head down studying. However, a few weeks into the year I realized this was something that wasn't going to go away so easily, and I was right.

One dreary day, in those shadowy dull corridors, it started. I was pushed around, into lockers, toilets, books knocked out of my hands, it felt like an effort to just simply walk down the corridor each day to my locker, get my books and walk to class. I had no idea what I would be facing or who. One day my life was 'invisible' and unimportant to everyone, the next day I was living in one of those teen movies, you know those ones where there's always that poor girl that a group insist on torturing with their teen angst crap. They belittle others, so they can make themselves feel good. I couldn't believe it, after watching it play out on screen so many times as a spectator I now felt like I was smack bang in the center of a Hollywood movie (where were the cameras?). Was someone just messing with me? It didn't appear so, I'd been thrown into the middle of 'whatever this was' without a heads up, and I had no idea what was happening. Each day my daily adventures of school bullying and embarrassment proceeded, and it was starting to get really nasty. I was being alienated further and now I hated school. Of course, I wouldn't tell anyone because I was always independent and fought my own battles. To make matters worse, and I'm sure just for shits and gigs my English teacher was failing me. He had some kind of vendetta between my brother and his friends back in the day, (my brother had long left school by now) so he thought he might just fail me, as you do, but not allowed to do as a teacher! It was quite obvious he had it in for me when my English grades plummeted from a B+ to an F which does not happen overnight, or over a summer. I didn't suddenly lose my brain in six weeks.

I got an idea what was going down here so I decided to set a plan in motion, a plan to expose him and the truth of why he was failing me for no reason. This was plan A, which was confronting him. Plan A didn't work, as he still denied everything, so my next step was Plan B, which was to get my mother involved along with the school Principle. My mother was like a warrior woman when you messed with her kids, so this was not going to be pretty. Note, hence why I did try to solve this one myself first, I did warn him. My mother marched my English teacher into the Principle's office and exposed his lies by forcing him to tell the truth, that he wasn't reading any of my papers but just marking an F when he saw my name. Which was the truth and he admitted it in front of us all, using me to get his revenge on my brother. This was silly because it didn't harm my brother; he was off having a lovely adult life now whilst I was getting the crappy grades. How was that getting back at him, it wasn't. However, he was made to re-grade all my papers and 'surprise' – I was back up to my B+/A pass. I wasn't sure what was more exciting, watching my mother take on my teacher in the principal's office or getting my high grades back. She was amazing and definitely set an example showing me that standing up for yourself, was a necessary evil. Go Mum!

As each day passed it became increasingly challenging to go to school, I was struggling. I had not told my family or confided in anyone at school that I was being bullied. Of course some knew, as they could see it occurring, but I was trying to keep it to myself and fight my own battles. Part of me felt weak if I couldn't do it myself, which was a very silly way to feel but hence why I didn't seek help.

Each morning I would check in to see if I could feel him walking with me, I could faintly still feel him but no answer or guidance did I feel coming through. I'm sure he was trying, in fact I knew he would be, there was no way he would leave me alone considering what I was facing, but I was too consumed in the world around me by now and had shut myself down. I wouldn't say I was anywhere in a centered or balanced state anymore and my mind was taking over. My days of having time to myself seemed far less than the days when I was young. As I grew older, they filled up with more 'stuff' fear, judgments, worries, concerns, bullying, protecting myself, all those things our mind tells us to be afraid of. Add to that the higher level of education studies and homework, boyfriend, friends and job. It was easy to see why entering adolescent years screwed people up even greater living more from their ego mind and less heart and soul. Was there any time left for any type of meditation or quiet time, not really. Mum was doing yoga which was close, it was relaxing, breathing, connecting, being centered and balanced. I probably should have joined her but there just never seemed enough hours in the day, and life appeared so complicated at present.

Of course there will never be enough hours available unless we make the time for ourselves – We all need balance in our lives, and this was something I wish I knew more about.

My home life wasn't particularly going well either, home where I sought that lovely shelter and quiet, to be myself had become more like walking on eggshells. My parents had a business that was currently causing them major stress, and it was filtering into our home life. The energy had become tense at times and each night we never really knew what we would be walking into. Seeing them stressed constantly, which was now causing them to argue regularly, was extremely hard for us. My beautiful father had lost his sparkle, he wasn't the same anymore. Those earlier happier days seemed few and far between now. Sometimes, one of the hardest things about being a teenager is feeling helpless to be able to emotionally and financially help your family. So as each day clocked over, I never really knew what to expect. Of course, at the end of a school day, I could go home, away from the bullies. In these school days, at least, we could remove ourselves from the bullying once our school day had finished.

My family were such beautiful honest people, and I hated seeing this happen to them. My brother, although, was now independently free, he still resided at home, but having his own wheels meant times had changed. He was working, going out with friends, doing what boys do, there were more people (his friends) coming and going in the house as our home sort of became the 'half way house' to anyone that needed to escape their own. It was different times. I was enjoying it, but it was just a different feel. We had grown up and more people had entered our world. My parents, although, having part of *their world* fall apart, still created that safe loving environment for others, and not only did they welcome so many into our home, they always joined in with us teenagers as well, having fun, which was really beautiful to watch. I felt blessed that I had parents who understood teenagers and wanted to join in with our friends, bringing them into our world, our home, where many other parents wouldn't do that, many others were glad when their kids went out.

When I could I spent most of my spare time in my room, not doing much of anything really but just to be alone. I had moved deeper into a place of solitude, in my heart. I was becoming numb losing more and more pieces of myself, but the yearning and longing to be me was so powerful. As I became more implanted in my world, the strangest thing started to happen, I felt like I was being pulled back to the other. It was like someone had a rope attached to me pulling me back each time I got a little too far off track. I would be tugged at like a magnet drawing me in, along with the sense of knowing that pull and the power in that pull, which reminded me who and what I knew myself to be. I don't think I ever stopped feeling like I lived between two worlds, as bizarre as that may sound, even with getting older and more in my ego, I still felt it. It was just always there and something I got used too. It had closed up more over the years but it never left me, I could always feel it but just not as clear. Of course, if you have never had this experience, it probably sounds rather silly, but it was real. As real as I was! I still questioned why I remembered when others didn't and in the real world, our world, the feeling of something missing still remained. I'd lived with this my whole life now, and I couldn't wait to wake up one day and not feel like half of me was missing anymore. It wasn't a nice feeling, but one day, hopefully, it would change.

I now spent time on weekends with my boyfriend, and occasionally, during the week, I had discovered males like my first real boyfriend were rare. He treated me very respectfully where others had not. My previous experiences had definitely been upsetting to say the least. I had been disrespected several times and dumped after a week sometimes because I wouldn't put out, and by put out I mean have sex. I wasn't frigid in any way but that didn't mean; I was about to put out just because they wanted it, I honored myself to wait till I was ready and to wait for the right person. This was one area of my life I wasn't prepared to just go along with what other's wanted me to do, so I could fit in. I had been exposed to the most incredible love my whole life, so I was way ahead of the game when it came to how I felt about someone or what was sacred. And I felt it right to my core. I didn't understand boys, or why they treated girls like they did, but I was not about to get pushed into anything just to make them happy. These experiences didn't exactly put males in a nice light for me. Why would they not want to respect girls? I didn't get it? I must have viewed relationships the old fashion way because I required respect. Perhaps, it's all in the way males are raised, and I have to say my boyfriend must have been raised well, because he knew exactly how to treat a girl, and he never tried to push me into anything I wasn't ready for. I knew I would carry some scars from my experiences for a while yet to come, and perhaps, this taught me to shut down my heart even more. I was slowly becoming the queen who was building a fortress around her heart.

I was aware escaping into a relationship was not the answer. Yes, it fills the voids, cover's the pain for a while, even feels good because it takes your mind off things, but it only causes further disconnection from yourself and in the long run more problems for you. It tends to feed your problems when you do this. This wasn't the case with my boyfriend or why I went back with him. I enjoyed being with him, and he made me feel comfortable to be around, he was relaxed, calm, gentle, nurturing, and extremely easy going which made our relationship a lot easier on me, as he never pressured me for anything or to be anyone, just to be me. I felt lucky to have him, given what I had been exposed to out there, as I never saw many like him. He became my first (physical) love.

Although I had him to talk to, I never opened to express my unhappiness. Truth is I wasn't in a happy place with my life, and I have no idea why I couldn't tell anyone. I was at my lowest – to the outside world, my life seemed fine, but inside, I was a mess. What was I missing? What was I not seeing? Interpretation is not always seen by the naked eye. A wise soul yes, but if one does not connect into that wise soul, they can't foresee the answer and obtain clarity in the truths. What was the truth, a world that was indignant led by the brain or one abundant and flourishing led by love, heart, and soul? Were people really this cold, rude, and cruel or was it a way we had been taught to release our aggression, pain, fear? Either way I had no idea, but sitting in my own little room trying to process what the hell was wrong with this world, and the people in it, was not getting me anywhere accept further down the rabbit hole of wonder. Maybe we needed to fall to understand it, or do most bury it behind an active ego.

I had experienced situations and events by this age that had affected me, things I had kept secret to everyone. I wasn't myself and contributing factors like the school bullying, along with not being able to feel my energy friend, who was always there to help me in crisis mode, were only escalating the situation. I had shut down to pretty much everything. For the first time in my life, I felt completely numb. I had never been able to open up to anyone and still couldn't. I learnt to solve everything myself or to get through but not this time, I felt lost to the point of no return. I didn't just get to this point overnight, nor in a few days. It was something that had built from school and my notion that I would never fit in no matter how hard I tried. My belief that I needed to, and my anxiousness knew I would never. One night after school, sitting in my bedroom, I started to ask myself. Did I want to stay in this world?

I was emotionless, staring at the wall, I couldn't do it anymore, and I had no desire to continue. The bullying had tipped me over the edge. Sitting at my desk, I pulled out a large note pad along with a pen and started to write a letter. A goodbye letter to my family!

No one had a clue I felt this way or wore many masks to cover up. But inside, I didn't want to be here anymore. After trying my best to contend with the bullying and pulling myself out of my slump, I was tired of trying to fit in whilst feeling such an outcast. I was tired of not being myself. I didn't want to go through years of being rejected, treated like I was a nuisance, by certain people, or weird because I didn't always say or do what 'normal' people did. But mostly, I was so sensitive, incredibly sensitive, that I struggled massively 'in silence' to accept people's criticism of me without taking it to heart. I was naïve, I thought everyone should just love or like each other and be kind. I was way too sensitive for this world, and I knew it. It drove me to fear lots, to wear these stupid masks and to try fill voids in places I had no idea how too. I was extremely empathic which only fueled the situation; empaths do struggle more than most. I was also struggling more now that my energy friend had gone, but even when he was around, it was a struggle to not have him in the physical world with me. It always seemed like half of me was someplace else. I truly didn't feel I could continue on in my life feeling everyday like I did. To me, if I didn't feel whole, it was pointless. I gave up waiting.

I always knew true love existed and I would have it, I would find 'The One' or he would find me. That one person that matched me perfectly.
I could feel it.
It was a knowing deep within my heart, a knowing imprinted upon my soul, a knowing I was destined to remember.

Chapter 13
The Knowing of Soul Love

On my journey, for as long as I could remember, I had carried a knowing that true love exists. I knew someone was out there for me; I never doubted. I knew certain people were connected with a love so profound that not all experience. We often hear the saying: 'if you find that one person in the world that is your soulmate, don't let them go.'

I didn't know exactly how the soulmate thing worked at the time because a soulmate could also be your friend, parent, sibling, family member, but we are guided to believe a 'romantic' soulmate is the one and only, often dubbed 'The One'. When people found their 'ONE', their world would light up, and it would become clear to all others around them.

I didn't believe we had more than one 'true love' out there; I knew there was only one person that was 'our one'. I also believed if you had a soulmate and were meant to be together in this lifetime, the universe would bring you both together. You would find each other. I also believed (and knew from my experience) the love talked about with soulmates could vary depending on the type of connection. Some had a stronger love than others.

I had no idea about anything else at this stage, only that my energy friend's love was much deeper again, because we felt not as two, but joined as one. My awareness of love was of a much more profound love than anything shown in movies, on TV, or in person. It was a love so deeply embedded and endless in my heart and soul. Not that I wish to place judgment on anyone's love but growing up as a spectator whilst feeling the love I was so blessed with, looked to me that most or pretty much everyone loved from conditional love. It never looked very unconditional to me. Often, it appeared more like a burden for most people. They seemed to be more tolerating of each other than loving each other, and it looked painful. I saw arguments, disagreements, lack of respect for one other. One or both filling voids they suffered in their life, hoping the other would fill them and fix all their problems. Most people that walked across my path fitted into this category, and I wondered, *was this as good as it gets on earth*. Because it, certainly, wasn't the love I'd felt to date, nor the love I felt from where I'd come from before entering this life. It didn't look very satisfying and blissful at all. Over the 'honeymoon period' of a relationship sure, but then it seemed more like people slipped into a 'settled comfort' state. It appeared people just chose who was around, who they bumped into rather than really searching for their true love, a bit like, 'you will do, you're here'. I could not think of anything sadder than living a life with someone in this energy, and I definitely couldn't see myself living like this.

My parents set a good example, as they were soulmates. Their loyalty, respect, and honor of each other were flawless and possibly the closet to unconditional love I ever witnessed in this physical world.

My intuition told me without a doubt I would find my true love one day and that when I met him, I would look into his eyes and know, instantly, it was him. I didn't doubt my intuition. However, did I really want to continue this painful journey alone until he arrived? Or did I want to go home?

***

When a teenager contemplates suicide, there can be various reasons which pushes us to this point, what triggers one may not trigger another. It's not about being weak or strong, being brave or courageous, it's not about what one can endure versus what another can't. It's about personal circumstances coupled with the outside world's perception. It doesn't matter what one knows, it's about what one 'feels'. **'Our perceptual field of limits created by those things around us and our society'** *along with the essence of who we are and how much we allow ourselves to feel, how sensitive, how much we actually feel versus someone not as sensitive. How empathic* *versus someone not all that empathic. Everyone is different, extroverts are more likely to express and speak up more than introverts – those teens that live inside themselves that may not share with those around them. No one really knows what will push a teenager to their limits or anyone contemplating suicide to be honest. We hope they will speak up; we hope they will ask for help but some of us don't. Sometimes, it takes others to really read the signs and pay attention, be vigilant, observe a person in their actions and really go that step deeper to ask, "Are you okay? I'm sensing something is not right." Anything, anything at all, that will show that person you're reaching out and ready to listen. That person may push you away at first, maybe continually, maybe ten times or more, but that doesn't mean you stop observing or checking on them. It doesn't mean you walk away saying under your breath, "well I've tried," and let them fend for themselves. It may take someone longer to open up and feel completely comfortable to express how they are feeling, to gain your trust and discretion. Usually, especially introverts, they won't want to share, they won't want anyone to know or make a fuss to start poking around. Introverts are silent warriors; we tend to fight our battles within 'alone'. We shut down thinking we don't need help; we can do this ourselves, but sometimes, we can't.*

There is always someone, some place, some other alternative out there to help us in every way. Someone that will show you love, compassion, and kindness, whose light shines bright like a beacon. You will feel these people, their beautiful energy. It may take discretion to find one but you will. Not everyone turns their back, not everyone leaves us to fend for ourselves, and there are many out there that do want to help. Reach out to those people and seek help, they are waiting, they may be in the form of a friend, a relative, a parent, a partner, a call center. You are never truly alone, they will always be shining their light for you, all you have to do is take that first step to ask.

***

No one in my world knew how I felt, let alone the thoughts of ending my life. There were signs, yes, but so subtle. I don't think I changed my appearance to those around me, I still acted as if I had it all together and wasn't showing my inability to cope. To share with another meant, I might have to share personal intimate information which I had never done in my past. Judgment became the monster I needed to face. I had tried, tried to let that fear go of being judged, but the truth was I never loved myself. I was judging myself, so of course, it opened the door for others to judge me too. I persevered but not hard enough, my energy friend had left me. (I knew in my soul he couldn't really leave me because we were attached somehow, but my ego was running the show at this point and depression had hit me.) I was done. I just couldn't do it anymore. For me it was like a switch flicked, and I was past the point of return. I'd had enough.

So back in my room I was compiling a letter to leave for my family, strangely enough with a complete sense of calmness around me. I finished writing, folded the letter and tucked it away in the envelope ready to leave on my desk. I put my pen down and reached out to start the process. I was literally a second away from doing what I'd planned, when an extremely loud 'male's' voice come out of nowhere and shook me to my core. I had heard it before. I knew this voice. I looked around my room because it was a voice in my physical world, not my head, but he wasn't there, no one was there. The sound had vibrated through my entire body, and I jumped. Where did his voice come from? He spoke words so loud, so clear, and precise.

"It is not your time to go, Kellie, you have to stay, you are here for a reason, for something bigger than you see right now, you can't leave. I am here…and I am 'coming'."

His voice was much louder than I ever recall, louder than I've ever heard, but the energy was the same. He was back, not that I could be sure he ever left. I had not actually ever heard his words that loud before, or heard them in the physical room with me, but this time it *was* a voice in my room not my head. He was surging through me with such incredible power and force, such determination to keep me on track. He sounded a little annoyed with me (not that I could blame him), he spoke very stern, and as he spoke his words, the energy changed as if he was taking over. In that moment, his energy and his voice was so incredibly powerful and protective, entering my body and taking over my physical actions. A power of protection I'd never felt before, which was new because I had felt his protection before, but this time, it was taken to a new level, this along with a beautiful calming, nurturing, loving energy telling me I had nothing to worry about. It was so extraordinarily powerful that it forced me to stop instantly, completely flipping my energy and every thought I had. I was clueless as to what was happening or how he was able to change everything in a split second. I just sat there in bewilderment while a wave of pure positive love and calming energy entered and uplifted my body. It coursed through me, erasing every negative thought, doubt, or fear I carried. It was the most unbelievable transition striking me with such force I really cannot explain. A force of his pure energy rapidly flooding every cell of my being and in that instant – I tore up the letter – not even realizing I had, almost feeling someone else did it for me.

I suppose it was my hands doing it, yes – but it felt like someone else's. I can't even begin to explain how everything shifted in that moment or fathom the chain of events, but everything had changed, and I was no longer considering taking my own life. Every thought and feeling around my impending suicide had vanished and the future looked brighter.

He was still with me, and he had just saved my life!

But who was he? And how did he have the ability to (without being in physical form) change my whole energy, my thoughts, perception, and my actions. He flipped my energy, took over entirely, and bestowed something so magical on me that wasn't possible for me to action myself. His energy was extraordinary, I was in amazement – there were no words. He was my beautiful savior!

When we surrender, it does open channels we never knew we had, light years away from any physical experience you could ever imagine, connecting to a higher source or power that does feel entirely magical in every way. To this day, I will never forget that moment and what that felt like for me. An unexplainable event that kept me here, kept me from leaving, and I am ever so grateful. His warm loving embrace was a god send, and I never wanted him to leave. His energy made it all feel so perfect. I didn't feel weird, different, or lost. It felt like home to me, it all felt perfect.

Reminding myself to feel him, connect into him, was something I would promise myself each day from now; and from this day onwards, I prayed each night that he would never leave or stop guiding me even knowing within, that he was a part of me. I was in affect praying that I could maintain the connection to myself, instead of living from a place of disconnection.

As I went over the events of that day, I wondered about his words.

"I am here, I am coming."

What did he mean? Was he trying to say he was coming like I had seen him, dreamed about? Was I to manifest him in my physical world like I had been trying my entire life, my soul constantly calling him in? Maybe he was due to come, or maybe he was already here living somewhere else, and I was connected to him, talking to him, telepathically. Perhaps, I would meet him soon, and this was why I knew one day I would be with my 'true love'.

That day woke me to the tremendous depth of this connection with my energy friend. After that day, I never doubted again that a much higher source of consciousness was guiding me throughout my life. All those previous feelings through my life of other universal worlds and paradigms beyond our human existence were real. Not that I ever doubted, but occasionally, it was easier to wonder was it all my imagination rather than believe in something that our human eyes could not see.

Chapter 14
My New Life Had Begun

As I seemed to accelerate to a higher level of perspective, I knew my only way around my school problem was to leave. As drastic as it was, I couldn't see any other way out. I suppose I could have talked to my teachers about the bullying but in the '80s if you did that, it often only created a greater problem on the school grounds, or outside school altogether. Dobbing (as we called it) was not an option. I had already stood up for myself by accepting a fight at school. I felt cornered with no way to back out, because by the time the invitation got to me it felt like half the school knew and were coming to watch. (I'm sure it wasn't half the school but it appeared that many were looking on) I felt pressured to fight this girl who had 'picked a fight' with me, otherwise more bullying would have continued. As I approached the 'scene', many thoughts were tumbling through my head of impending embarrassment if this all went her way and not mine. As a shy invisible girl, I was now placed out in front of many onlookers who were waiting to see which one of us would be humiliated in view of this large audience. I may have been trembling inside a little, not fearing her, but fearing others laughing at me if I lost. I knew facing that was much worse than facing her, so I had to win this fight. I had to approach it with all my 'superpower'. I could muster up within and attack with the warrior 'Aries' young woman. (I think the 'Wonder Woman' inside me was bubbling up to the surface ready to explode.)

We started and it was your typical bitch fight *no surprises there* scratching, punching, biting, pulling hair, rolling around on the grass, all so insanely immature and senseless, but at the time I felt if you can't beat 'em, join 'em. I do feel the person in question did underestimate me slightly, as when I get mad or pissed off enough, I can switch into top gear and not be so much the shy girl. She was shocked, and I was glad it was over. I may have surprised many on lookers too as the quite shy girl emerged into this powerhouse. Funny how people underestimate us quiet types. After that day, I know several would think twice before attacking a shy girl. I can definitely defend myself when needed.

The bullying (whilst not the only reason) was a contributing factor to why I felt pushed to my recent suicide attempt. Knowing I could not endure another two years of this, I decided school had to go. I discussed with my parents the possibility of leaving school if I secured a good job. My long time choices of nursing or being a flight attendant would be no longer, as I needed to graduate for those, but if I worked in an office as a secretary maybe I could work my way up. A secretary was not one of my choices in life, I never wanted to be stuck in an office, never imagined myself doing this. However, there were not too many choices available if you weren't a graduate. I had to look at what skills I possessed; science would do me no good unless I was headed to University. I had exceptional typing skills, so I applied for positions with those required skills. In the '80s, in Australia, university wasn't as high on everybody's list as it is today. You only stayed to year 12 and graduated if you desired to go to college, and you only went there if you wanted a profession that required a university degree. Anyone that wanted a trade left at the end of year ten, as most apprentice jobs recruited from year ten. The wages for an apprentice were low but it didn't really matter at this age as most still lived at home. I didn't want to be stuck in an apprentice wage for four years. Given these circumstances, it wasn't all that unusual I was leaving, only that for me I never planned to. So it was a surprise. I always wanted to graduate whether I went on to university or not. My plans had never involved dropping out of high school, and I knew I had the grades to go all the way. The bullying turned everything upside down for me and given the fact I had just attempted to take my own life, I felt leaving was the better option. University was something that did appeal to me; and if I decided to go, I was going to take a gap year anyway to backpack around Europe first, returning to start a degree, but now that had all changed.

My first priority was to create a life for myself that kept me from wanting to leave this world. School and University became secondary.

My parents agreed on me leaving school if I was to secure a good job, so I started applying. My second job interview was successful and my school days were over. It all happened so fast that I had to think the universe was aligning it perfectly. I walked out of school, not looking back, and walked into a secretary position in a realtor firm. My parents were a little shocked as they expected I may not secure a position at all, or at least, not as soon, but they allowed it and saw like me, that – the universe was at play. Perhaps, they saw this as the only way to keep me here (on earth) and why the alignment occurred so quickly. My new life was about to begin.

My typing skills were the reason I secured my position, never in a million years had I thought I would be using them. I had only taken that class as a backup; a 'just in case my career choices didn't manifest' backup. Looks like the universe knew something I didn't, because this 'for now' was obviously my path. *When the universe is at play, nothing stands in its way.*

Nervousness and pure relief overcame me. Was I really ready to start fulltime work along with responsibilities in this world, or was it all too soon? Not that I really had a choice. I felt I was being propelled into the unknown, and a life way off course to what I had dreamed of. I had a boyfriend, a fulltime job, and was starting my adult life at the sweet early age of 16.

My work skills having performed in a convenience store, rolling skating rink, and Supermarket, now were getting put to the test working 9–5 in a professional realtor office. In some way, my naïve approach to the transition had me pretending it wasn't a big deal. But I was about to learn otherwise. In one short leap, I felt like I was an adult, and I left many of my school friends behind in a decision that felt right. Who really prepares for something like this? Although, I felt like I was honoring myself. Maybe I had changed the path of my life, or maybe this was meant to be, who knew, but as we ebb and flow through life, it all unfolds often in a way we do not expect.

Sometimes we have to go off course to stay on track, as weird as that sounds.

Here, in this world, life can throw us numerous obstacles, and many of us believe we are here to learn lessons. I used to believe that but not anymore. I think the lessons we learn are the ones where we have veered off course or used our FREE WILL and EGO to create situations that ***do not*** serve us at all. The universe will always show us over and over again until we learn our mistake. If you are living the same cycle or pattern and you need to grow, it will show you in many different ways. The only way for us to grow and evolve is when we are pushed out of our 'old cycles' showing us they are no longer serving our heart or soul. I know my life could have deviated onto a different path and maybe that would have led me to myself quicker, or maybe this one I was on was where I needed to be. Who knew? But in a way, it felt right. I was a believer that if it's not to be the opportunity won't arise. The fact it all happened so quickly and with no employment experience, showed me this opportunity was created for me.

My belief is we are not here to learn lessons. I believe we are here to remember what we already know.

School taught me a lot of good things, but it also taught me that the world we live in can be a nasty judgmental place. It can be extremely negative, violent, fearful, and jealous. It really woke me up to the perplexity of it all. Imagine a school where we could all share love and peace, respect each other, and be kind. I don't propose to cast blame on others; they were merely living in the same times of adjustment, in a world transitioning rapidly and just trying to fit in, like I was. We all react differently to situations beyond our control. We also stem from our personality, the traits that see us resist or non-resist. What we allow or not allow.

The changing ways from the '70s to the '80s were extreme in many ways; those times were accelerating at a fast pace. Musician's influenced us, movies, political statements, and '80s society culture. In so many ways, it was exciting. I loved the change in music – the birthing of many new genres with completely different sounds like never heard before. Music was helping people get through these times; it was full of expression, statements, and heartfelt messages. Artists were inspired by social and political events and changes. Many made a point to bring awareness to the world through their inspiring lyrics, to show people they were not the only one feeling this way. It was evident that the '80s had a lot more to come and was on a mission to change the face of living, how we knew it to be. Television shows were now completely different than the days of the '70s. Movies were increasingly deeper and raw, starting to depict real life, social situations and difficulties, especially for teens. It did project an exciting energy, nonetheless, along with such change we didn't foresee.

From what I read about the hippie age generation (the one I was born a little too late for), they tried to bring a collective awareness protesting against war, citing love, peace, compassion, and kindness, and if only it flowed throughout the world as a phenomenon the world might not be in the mess it was, and is today. However, after a few years of trying, it seemed to slow down, and by the time I was a little girl, it appeared almost non-existent. Hippies tried to bring the 'new age' or 'spirituality' energy, the start of the Age of Aquarius, but unfortunately, it seemed to have proved to be a little before most of humanity was ready. Flower power had a beautiful message, and it wasn't anything to do with the drugs. Along with trying to wake up the world, they were trying to fit into a dense, controlled world with war and violence; these people knew we all should be united as a collective, spreading love and peace for all. Helping people to become conscious was a revelation before it's time, but set the foundations for the future.

Looking back now, I see myself more suited to that lifestyle, not that I was interested in the Psychedelic experience, I didn't need anything to open my perception to the 'real world' as I already had that connection, I saw quite clearly the differences how most lived or were living in this fake one, the one we humans reside in. But in many ways, I was living in that fake one as well, because I wasn't following my heart and higher guidance. It would have been nice to be around more awakened spiritual people that may have been able to help me on my path, to help me show the real me. I never really met anyone that was 'awake' in those times growing up, which if I did, I'm sure would have helped.

Chapter 15
Blessing or Curse

My life had tipped upside down in a very short time, and my head was spinning a little. It was all a new learning experience and people weren't wrong when they said:

"You know you're alive when you leave school and enter the adult world."

When you're suddenly out in the big wide world of adults, responsibilities, time cards, and lunch breaks (I did like those lunch breaks) takes a little getting used to. It was a world away from school – teachers, school books, and immature bullying. You transition over night to a mature world surrounded by money, business talk, and bosses.

I learnt how the world of Realtors worked – contracts, money, sales, rentals, marketing, and it was an eye opener. As I learnt the day by day saga of the Real Estate world and how it all operated, I could see, in some ways, I was learning valuable experiences for this world we live in. I learnt my job quickly and executed my duties well, however, did I like it? Enjoy it? Not particularly. I can't say I was over joyed or woke each morning full of excitement and passion to jump out of bed to go to work. Sitting at a desk was not what I had seen for myself. But considering this type of job was never really high on my list, it made sense that I lacked the passion.

The quote, *'Do what you love, love what you do'* wasn't really cutting it in this job.

As much as I put 100% into my work, I knew I wasn't cut out to be working in an office surrounded by four walls, doing a 9 to 5 working week. I chose it so I could leave school, it was a form of survival, but I knew it wasn't my passion. At 16, I hadn't found my passion yet, had anyone by that age? I had been told only recently that I was here for 'something special' but no more information was offered up when my beautiful energy friend told me this. He may have been a little too busy to share details whilst he was performing miracles to keep me alive, but still, a little more info on the situation may have been helpful.

I have learnt, years on, that we are not always told what we are supposed to be doing or what's happening with our future, because often we can change it. Just our free will, actions and thoughts, or our anxiousness and impatience can take us off path. This may be why I was not privy to any more information from the universe at the sweet age of 16.

Where I resided 'as beautiful' as it was, it was likened to a small country town where not too much happened. I wasn't from a big city like New York, Paris, or London, I wasn't subjected to the kind of people that where movers and shakers in the world or had those opportunities. My family was not well known, nor were they in positions of power or fame, and I didn't live in a city full of action. Because of this, I wondered how I was going to have the opportunity to make a difference in this world.

Writing was one of my passions, pouring out my heart to the blank pages of my diary was a release for me. It was therapy for an introvert. I wrote to the universe daily, asking for assistance and sharing my inner deep feelings. I asked several times if I promised to stay, would they please bring my friend, my love, into human existence for me, could they bring him into my world so we could be together both in human form. I prayed each night and hoped, if I did this on a regular basis, he would appear.

As the Astrological Zodiac signs go, I am an Aries. Aries women are fairly known for their power, strength, and bold fiery confident ways. They are passionate, independent, spontaneous, and self-reliant, they also like things done yesterday. (I was a true Aries when it came to liking things done yesterday, patience wasn't my virtue.) Aries females are also very creative in many ways and often enjoy challenges. I wasn't sure I fitted the mold completely to be honest, with all of these, but one thing I knew for sure was that I was creative, and creative people are not serving themselves or feeding their soul working in an office. I had figured this much out.

One of the beauties, however, of living in a coastal township was working opposite the beach. I was extremely grateful for the position of my employment, as it enabled me to walk directly across the road onto the sand. It was so close I could sit at my desk typing whilst looking out the window (between the pictures) to view the water. Each day for my lunch break, I would take myself across the road to sit by the beach, just by myself, relaxing in solitude whilst soaking up the peacefulness. Watching the seagulls flying around, admiring the sun sparkling on the water, and the ripples as they expanded far out to sea caused by the comings and goings of fishing boats – this I loved. I loved watching the older fisherman throwing their lines in from the pier and their excitement when they reeled in another fish, the few brave swimmers bracing the chilly waters, and the couples strolling hand in hand along the pier. I sat thinking what a beautiful place to live. However, I knew someday I would leave as there was more to this planet I craved to embrace, but those moments in time were serene, and I needed them in my *every* day. Venturing out for lunch with these surrounds didn't make me feel quite as suffocated, bounded by the four walls of the office, it was definitely the relief I needed.

My boyfriend and I worked in the same town, although he wasn't as lucky as I was to work opposite the beach, he wasn't far away, so he would pick me up after work and drive me home. It was nice being collected and greeted after work with his smiling face, and this was something I could look forward to throughout my day. I never really felt like I fitted in at work and I still felt I had been catapulted into a strange world. *Well I suppose that wasn't anything new.*

Life was moving along okay, but sadly, I hadn't been feeling my beautiful friend all that much. In my peaceful moments, by the beach, I could feel his energy with me, but again, silence. He hadn't spoken to me since that day. My work didn't help as it had catapulted me more into the materialistic world, and although I was close to my boyfriend, I never shared with him that real me, inside, or my energy friend.

My boyfriend had a beautiful balance of masculine and feminine energy, quite balanced in both actually, he wasn't aggressive or egotistical, and he had a lovely personality/nature. Sometimes, he probably was a little too much on the 'go with the flow' side, but I rather liked that. I was his first love and him mine, I don't think either one of us knew much about love or what true love was, but we had each other. I knew how amazing 'Love energy' was through my experience with my friend, but again I hadn't seen that love in this physical world, so I wondered if that existed here.

I think when we are young, life takes us on journeys with others to experience different love connections. We often have to be with others to learn about love, so when our real, true love comes along we know with every beat of our heart, that person is 'The one', and it's maybe just my perception, but I wonder, if we didn't have those experiences, then would we know for sure? I'd been shown such pure incredible love from a very early age, and I think any love would struggle to come close to that.

Watching my family struggle before my eyes, as everything they had worked for was slowly slipping away, was heartbreaking and painful. I'd gradually lost my dad a little more each day under the stress they endured. They worked so hard to hold onto everything only for it to be ripped away by an outside source. It would only be a matter of time before we would have to sell our home, our beautiful home I loved, that was my sacred place, the only home I had really known. I had this new job but my earnings were very little, they weren't anywhere near enough to help make a dint in my parent's financial situation, it was far beyond anything my brother and I could help them with. I hated seeing this happen to our family; I hated watching their hearts break a little more each day, but I vowed the day would come where I would be so wealthy enough to buy my parents a new home.

In life, we 'settle' for things. 'Settle' in relationships, 'settle' in jobs, 'settle' for many things we are not in love with, but like anything in life we 'settle' for, it will have an expiration date because there is only so long we can pretend or load another mask on top. I was 'settling' with my job as it really wasn't for me, but to make matters worse I was thrown into a situation beyond my control causing me to keep yet another secret. My days at the realtor were numbered, as it was becoming increasingly difficult to avoid a work situation. I was secretly hiding the fact that I was being sexually assaulted by one of my managers. It started about one month into my employment when one morning we ended up alone together in the kitchen, I was making the morning round of coffees for each employee, as I normally did, and he appeared over my shoulder. This was one of my daily jobs, so it was difficult to avoid being in the kitchen for morning tea, and he knew that. Each time he crept up and suddenly appeared behind me with his groping hands. I tried to fight back his advances, but each time I tried to tell him no or push him away, he threatened me. As the days and weeks passed by, he continued to touch me in ways that exceeded his initial groping, and I was beside myself. Each time I pushed him away or tried to get away, he would not hesitate to remind me that not only would he have me fired, but his influence in this town/peninsula would serve to never see me in a job again. So If I wanted future employment, I best comply. I became numb. I know it sounds absurd that I would stay to endure such treatment, but all I could think of was what would my parents say if I was fired, and would I have to go back to school to face the bullying. In some preposterous way, I was fighting for my survival as well and both options were equally shocking. Men exert their power, I was 16 and scared to death, I used my voice, but it didn't stop him. In the '80s, sexual harassment in the workplace wasn't really discussed, it was another 'secret topic' that women were scared and bullied into being silent for fear of losing their jobs or worse. With some men, it's a power play used from their position to intimidate a woman. I felt shame, scared, and powerless. If I was fired, would I get another job? If I didn't have a good working reference, he surely wasn't going to give me one, or would I be labeled a liar (as he told me he would deny it), and therefore, would anyone else hire me. Small town, people talk. I felt so violated, dirty, cheap, and I struggled to understand what was wrong with me.

As this went on for months, with maybe the exclusion of a few days here and there when he wasn't working, it had started to affect my work and was becoming noticeable. His wife worked in our office as well, and I could see she started to look at me differently, so I figured she was suspect to his actions. And I wondered how many others he may have done this to. I had a feeling I wasn't the first one and maybe he already had a history that she was privy too. As time went on, my enthusiasm for the job, plus the thought of coming to work to face him each day had declined, but I still maintained a high level of work. However, out of the blue one day I was dismissed with the explanation that I was starting to make typing errors. This was incorrect as my typing skills had always been exceptional; I could type 100 words per minute with 98% accuracy and had been able to do this since 9th grade. My fingers flew across those keys so efficiently that it was completely ridiculous to use this as an excuse. Typing was something I excelled at. However, I never questioned my termination as such relief engulfed me when I heard those words; and for the moment, I never even worried about future employment. But the strangest thing happened after firing me, they followed it up with, "But we have found you a new job, if you want it," and it was to commence the following week. It was the most bizarre situation, being fired, but them finding me new employment at the same time. It was obvious I was being 'set free' and this was some kind of 'apology' for what they realized was occurring. I'm sure it was also a nice way of saying, "Look no hard feelings because we have found you a new job, so you can now keep your mouth shut." And I did…

Nine months after I walked into my first full-time position, I was walking out; from that day on I wondered if my body was a *'blessing or a curse'*.

Chapter 16
Scars

The scars I now wore were etched deep, and the thought had crossed my mind if my beautiful male energy love helped me. I had felt powerless to stop what was happening to me, to report him, out of fear of his threats. Instead, I had shut down and numbed myself to the situation; but in the end, it was like someone reached in and took it all out of my hands, because I couldn't. I wondered if it was him, he always stepped in to protect me or change the path when I needed, and I was still feeling very guided by him. Although he was still in silence and not speaking, 'as he hadn't since that day in my room', I could feel him with me and I always knew when he had taken over. That day there was no question in my mind. And if only I was open more and not so numb, I may have been able to here his words. Why didn't he speak loud to me again? Why would he not? Would it not be so easy for him to tell me what to do? I guess I had to stand on my own two feet and not rely on him so much…it scared me a little…was there a day coming where I had to walk alone? And would I stay in this world if I did?

My ego said: "You can't go on living your life being guided by spirit, that's not taking responsibility yourself."

But on the other hand I knew it was right, that there was a higher force to help us, guide us throughout this thing we call life. Especially, when you experienced it being an extension of yourself.

My heart whispered: "Where are you? Are you in there still? Why can't I hear you anymore? Why won't you speak to me? Did I do something wrong?"

When I needed help or struggled, he was stronger; when I needed love, it was euphoric; when I needed guidance, I was always guided; and when I opened up to him, he became stronger. But there was something I was doing to stop him, pushing him away. When I fell unconscious and resisted my higher knowing or abilities, it would elude me. I was trying so extremely hard to feel him but at the same time, 'was I opening to receiving him?'

It appeared a greater percentage of the world's population were not living from a higher perception, (back then and today). This would be why they couldn't feel or see energy, or anything other than what they could physically see in front of them. We often need that little reminder that – Energy IS Everything!

Spirituality

Spirituality is not religion, spirituality is not about following the masses being told what to believe in, it's about going within, connecting yourself, and having your own experiences. Spirituality unites the world through love; it does not divide or separate. Spirituality chooses from love not fear. It's about experiencing yourself at your 'higher self' soul level by way of connecting all three 'mind, body, and spirit', finding within the true essence of who you are as a soul, finding the real you. When we connect to this higher self, consciousness, frequency, we receive the greater picture of who we truly are, where we come from, what our purpose is here and a universal consciousness as one. It's an awakening to all, evolving beyond a limited mind perception of the lower human vibration, and through this personal growth we achieve and align with a greater love – self-love...*unconditional love*...our purpose, gratitude, and abundance. When we are in connection with ourselves fully understanding the path we are on, and why we are here, fully releasing all fears, doubts, insecurities, and pain, we can push through to live the most incredible evolved state of BEing. Awakening, we also see very clearly the world around us, and choose to live our lives no longer from that lower vibrational state of fear. Spirituality is about raising our consciousness; and when we do, we see the lower paradigm we

145

have been taught and guided to live within. When this occurs, one becomes more centered, balanced, and shifts into living from their heart and soul, and less from fear or their ego mind. When this occurs we feel the sense of peace and freedom that most only dream about. Our life fills with love and opportunities, happiness and most importantly living from truth in all ways. It doesn't mean our 'ego' won't try to raise up and pull us down again with a negative thought or feeling, we are all human; but at this point, you will have the awareness, and awareness is key to being able to shift out of that lower vibration when that occurs.

Despite the fact that life is quite different these days with so many of the collective waking up and leading a more healthier state of being and living from a higher awareness. Back then, people thought you were weird or something was wrong with you if you tried to live this way. Over the last few decades with the gentle push from those aware and integrating spirituality further into their world, coupled with the earth's rising frequencies, have helped many to rise up and start to awaken. Spirituality is becoming more mainstream now, and so we can look back on those times then and see it was definitely starting to path the way for today.

'Humans fear what they do not understand.'

From my own experiences and what I remembered coming into this life, this is what I believed:

I believed in Soulmates, the ultimate love, the afterlife or life after death as some would say. I knew I was not from here, as I have already explained, I knew I was from a far greater place of love and infinite light and our time on earth was short, along with a purpose, experience and soul maturity (depending on your soul) I also knew, because of this, once we completed our journey here, we were going back home. So I never feared that death was it, over and out. I didn't have any other answers, and I couldn't really explain to anyone how I knew this, I just did. Call it a remembrance. I believed that if people died young it was often *but maybe not always* because they had fulfilled their purpose or their 'contract' of life at this time, and I knew that not all of us were here to make it to 100. I believed the people that crossed our path were meant to be there and serve a purpose; also that some may stay a short time, a long time, or a lifetime. I knew the ones that were meant to stay would. I knew and believed in past lives, I had 'way too many occurrences happen' where I recognized I had 'done this before' or 'already known that'. I had visions, sometimes, like a projector screen flash in front of me, and I knew things I could not possibly have known in this life already. I also believed, somehow, we all had a contract agreed upon before we transitioned into this physical world. I guess overall I brought a knowing with me that some others had not remembered, but yet I had hidden this from all around me most of my life.

I listened to several people over time that didn't quite believe there was life beyond; some thought that once your time was up it's up. Others did question, hoping there was some kind of life after, and many never talked about this topic at all. We are all here having our own experiences, created by ourselves, and like I said, everyone is here for something different. When you are here on a mission or a specific purpose – you will know it, the universe will always be helping you to that, and on to that path, and one thing you will realize is, *the universe never gives up*.

Chapter 17
Loss, Love, and Growth

As time moved on so did the '80s, I considered (at one point) going back to school to graduate but realized that ship had sailed. I was grateful I already had more experience in the work place than anyone I knew my age, and experience was a valuable asset. Besides, I was enjoying life with my own money and independence. I don't think I ever really unleashed my true self; the masks stayed on so long it sort of gave me a false sense of who I was. I began to believe this was me, and as conflicting as it was, I had convinced myself well. I didn't know if I would ever live from my truth or if I would ever get past the fear of judgment from others if I did. In some way, it was easier pretending, although, I was to see it did not feed my soul in any way, and I was still empty.

Owning a home became important to me after witnessing my parent's losses, so as much as I wanted to save for my Europe backpacking vacation, I had purchased a piece of land (when I was working at the realtors) with my current boyfriend. So at the age of 16, I owned my first piece of land. I must say unless I worked in Real Estate I probably wouldn't have considered buying at this point, but I had learnt how lucrative investing in property was. I almost purchased two beach boxes on the foreshore as well for a very inexpensive price of 1,000 dollars, but changed my mind at the last minute. (This wasn't my finest decision!) My boyfriend and I were going well, but I realized he wasn't remotely interested in traveling. I still had my heart set on Europe, but he didn't seem keen. He was a real homebody, and I wasn't sure how this would pan out. Would I end up giving up my dream of Europe or would I still go on my own. The piece of land we purchased was not necessary to build a home upon, it started out as an investment, but I had not ruled out in the future maybe we would. I wasn't sure what the future held for us, and I was too young to rush into anything. When we were together, at times, I felt my energy friend, but I kept the feeling to myself. I never shared, it became part of me that was between 'us' and I took on the guidance from him when I felt him guiding. I still secretly asked him to come be with me and was awaiting the universe to guide me to this 'reason' I was here, that I had to stay for.

***

Christmas was approaching, and it was that time of year again to select the Christmas tree. Each year, for as long as I can remember, my mother would 'choose' a tree that she had her eye on for months selected from around the area she worked 'up on the hill'. She prided herself on her Christmas tree; Christmas was her favorite time of year and the tree had to be perfect. So in the car, we would go to travel to get this Christmas tree, and she would just about drive my father crazy. It wasn't just remembering the 'spot or paddock' the tree was in, it was the conversation that started once we stopped. Mum would point the tree out to dad and the discussion from then on was the following, the same conversation they would have each time, every year.

Dad: "That tree is too big for the house; it won't fit through the door."

Mum: "Oh, yes it will, of course it will, it's not that tall."

Dad: "I'm not cutting down that tree because it won't fit; you will have to choose another one."

Mum: "It will fit, I'm telling you it will fit fine, it looks beautiful, and it's perfectly shaped, I want that one."

Dad: "If we take that tree home and it doesn't fit in the living room, if it's too high for the ceiling, I will have to cut the top of the tree off, then it won't look so beautiful."

Mum: "Okay, let's choose another tree, I'm not cutting the top off, that will look ridiculous."

So then on to the next lot of paddocks we would go for her 2nd and 3rd choices. It was such a funny time as it happened every year, same conversation – same outcome. But her excitement and the sparkle in her eyes about a tree, and decorating for Christmas was so beautiful to watch. We would have the biggest tree with hundreds of lights and decorations and each year I must say it looked so perfectly shaped.

Summers are different when working as opposed to being in school as of course I didn't get summer holidays. That was the part I missed. But as we had Day Light Savings time in Australia, it made the days longer and the nights shorter, so I still experienced my beach times and other enjoyable activities after work and on the weekends. Two of my older cousins had asked if they could move down from the city and live with us, and as accommodating as my beautiful parents were, of course they said yes. Now I was living in a house with 3 older guys, plus my boyfriend would come over so often I felt I was surrounded by males, but I loved it. They were easier to talk to than females. We all had partners, we were working, and we intermingled our lives on weekends with fun activities. We had increased our family through the kindness of my parents, even under the financial stress they were enduring. My parents loved hanging out and having fun with us all, my dad got along with all the boys and often we would all go camping together up to the river.

Camping river side was so peaceful, I wasn't super keen on the 'makeshift' bathroom, literally in the bush, but it was definitely the most rural camping experiences I had in my life. When you wake to the stillness of the river and the sounds of the birds, the smell of mother nature (unless dad had started cooking the bacon and eggs on the BBQ) in which case you could only smell breakfast, but in all honesty, there is nothing better than connecting to nature and being still long enough to appreciate it. We didn't care what we looked like, brushing our hair and makeup wasn't anywhere in sight, it was so natural and raw, and we all loved it. Dad would always take his boat and back it into the river for us to fish. We had a few joyrides in the cars, a little bit of 'bush bashing' which as I recall, one car ended up half in the river on one visit, but those days were far away from the daily grind of the matrix, and I loved them. We would have family, friends, and partners, with nights sitting around the campfire playing guitar and singing, or good conversation while toasting marshmallows, these were some of my highlights. I hold beautiful memories of those days camping by the river.

Christmas had passed, and we were well into the New Year when something incredibly unexpected and frightening was about to rock our world. We were about to endure a life altering experience for all of us in different ways.

***

There comes a time in our life where we are faced with a situation of possibly losing a loved one, and this was no exception, only it was four.

In the face of our worst bushfires in history blazing through our state my brother, boyfriend, and my two cousins (my new brothers) were called up to fight the fires, all being members of our local fire brigade. Within 12 hours more than 180 fires fanned by 110km/h winds spread throughout our beautiful state.

One by one we kissed them goodbye as we watched them leave the house to all be posted to different fire trucks and locations, and the fear was overwhelming. We couldn't help but fear if we would see them again, as we knew what they were stepping into. Reports had already shown some fire fighters had died whilst fighting the blazes; all we could do was be extremely positive, hopeful, and pray. But it was incredibly difficult! It doesn't matter how positive you try to be your mind is ticking over with that thought, *what if they don't return, what if I never see them again.*

We waited anxiously for each one to return praying the fires were under control, so they didn't have to go back again, but they were only back to rest, eat, sleep whilst the changeover of shift, than back up to do it all over again. Days felt like weeks and as each one left I pretty much held my breath for their safe return. As each one returned, we heard stories first hand from the front line and could see the devastation on their faces as they explained and the proof on their blackened uniforms. We scanned the news updates regularly and when it reported a recent volunteer fire brigade platoon were all taken by the fire, it was the scariest thing to hear. Sitting from our living rooms we watched as they showed the fire raged out of nowhere, so fierce and changing course, and because of this, had caught them fully unexpected. The truth is we knew it could have happened to anyone of those fire trucks out there, and that reality hit home even more brutal. The winds were changing the direction of the fires at any time, forcing fire fighters and residents to be caught, as the flames were rolling over the hills higher than you could ever imagine.

At that age, we think we are invincible, we often don't foresee anything bad could happen to us or our loved ones. That day – over that period, was my greatest reality check that disasters can affect anybody. We could only *try* to imagine the fear these young brave men were facing as they left and returned. It was far greater than anything we were feeling. We remained a comfort for them upon their return, listening as they feared the worst, and their life flashed before their eyes but had got lucky, times they almost got caught but miraculously escaped, and we all felt in our own way that someone was looking out for our family.

Relief is such an understatement of what we all felt when those intense days were over and they returned home safe, but some sadly were not so lucky. We almost lost one of ours in a very hairy moment, and for his safe return we were so incredibly grateful. Those fires took the lives of 17 fire fighters across our small state, destroyed many homes, animals, and wildlife. Our boys were part of the lucky ones, and we thanked god with much gratitude for their safe return.

***

The experience I faced impacted me severely, and I started to think about life. What I really desired for myself and how to achieve that. Circumstances were changing around me, and it was a time of not only adjustment but reflection.

My parents lost their home after a battle to try and hold on for so long, along with our beautiful boat – that was my dad's pride and joy, and which we spent all those fun days on the water fishing, laughing, and spending time together. One by one not only did my parents lose everything they had worked so hard for, but I saw the light go out in my dad. He was broken hearted, in some ways there was relief for him not bearing the financial burden any longer, but in other ways it was devastating for them. Health and family always come before material possessions, no question. However, to see all you have acquired in your life to be taken away before your eyes, does something to a man. I felt helpless; I didn't know what to do for my parents... And I was fairly mad at the universe!

As the world turns, we say one door closes, another opens. Well I couldn't see the other opening as yet, all I could see was complete heartbreak for my family. We had to move. Leaving our home was one of the hardest things we had to do, and I was lost in how I felt about the whole thing. It was the only home I remembered, and it was now gone. It not only broke my parent's heart...it broke mine as well.

So many memories in this home, it was my safe, sacred place with my energy friend and nothing felt the same anymore. Although I knew he would come with me as he had done all my life, and I also understood that it didn't matter where I lived, because he's in me somehow, but that wasn't really the point. We had so many precious memories there. My father lost his passion with life and my mother was trying hard to keep everything composed, they were so in love which I'm sure was the only glue that held our family together. There had been many fights and arguments under the pressure, and I saw firsthand how this world could *'chew you up and spit you out'*, no matter how hard you tried. Mixed feelings inside about all I saw only proved to discourage me more about living in this world. The very things that controlled our lives were the things we couldn't live without. Money, a home, food, employment, that was my first glimpse of how becoming an adult pushed you into a world that swallows you up. A world that survives on money, greed, power, and control, along with laws, society rules, and standards. It all made me sick to see how it could destroy people, destroy humanity. But I think the worst thing I realized was how it controlled us, or at least projected the illusion that it did. It caught everyone in a web of limited beliefs and fears, not realizing there were other alternatives of living, not realizing just how addictive life became to live with all these material items, and advanced new technologies. As I looked around, I could see just about everyone being programmed to the same station, with the view that life had to be this way. Yet, what I viewed on my previous overseas holiday was a different reality, island living of less material needs and wants and a more relaxed simple way of existence equaled *Love, kindness, caring, and peace*.

***

I spent the latter part of my teenage years employed, relatively happy, still with my boyfriend and hanging out with others doing the normal things. I really had no idea what I wanted to do with my life in terms of being happy at work or anything else, but I did know I still wanted to travel to Europe. It was the popular thing in my generation that we left school and went backpacking around the UK and Europe and that's all I wanted to do. Maybe secretly I was going in search of my missing piece, or that person I knew to be out there, because let's face it, what were the odds I would find him living in my sleepy little town?

Traveling overseas to Fiji along with the excitement of 'Summer Lovers' – 'Santorini', ignited the travel bug in me and there was no turning back. I knew I definitely wanted to see more of the world, many different walks of life, cultures, adventures, incredible nature, and breathtaking scenery; I wanted to explore our planet and see how others lived.

After some discussion about traveling, excitement brewed and a group of us decided to book a P&O cruise on an 18–35s itinerary around the South Pacific Islands. Our departure date arrived, and we all flew to Sydney to set sail that afternoon off into the sunset. Excited and ready for some fun, lots of partying and nightclubbing on board and not to mention more visits to the islands. These visits brought even more insight to their beautiful traditional culture, food, nature, and a relaxed stress free life.

We enjoyed the ship lifestyle of docking in ports each day to take in the sites or stay on the boat and enjoy the relaxed days by the pool. I was always keen to disembark at ports and tour around taking in the Islanders culture, meeting the locals, and breathe in the simplicity. I didn't enjoy being around lots of people that much, so putting myself out there for meet and greets were difficult for me, but I loved their natural friendly vibe and chilled lifestyle. I was in love with these lifestyles beyond our fast pace of living. It fed my soul in a beautiful way and opened me up to more.

Upon returning home, I was starting to see my life now in a different way, I had matured further and nothing seemed to feed my soul. I didn't want marriage, kids, a house, although my ego was having a fine conversation trying to convince me I did. I was young (although I felt ancient). I wanted to experience life in all its fun and glory, settling down felt wrong to me. My ego was telling me one thing, and my heart and soul another. However, for some reason beyond comprehension before I knew it I had become engaged at the tender age of 17. How did that happen? Not that my boyfriend wasn't a lovely guy and I did love him, but I had made the wrong choice to become engaged. We both had, we both wanted very different things in life, but I'm not quite sure if we could both see it so clearly at that time. In fact, I think because we loved each other we resisted seeing it, for maybe the comfort of staying together.

***

We were almost half way through the '80s and so far it had bought with it a pop culture that would be long talked about in the history books. Several changes had occurred by way of lifestyles; in fact, it was shaping up to be the most talked about decade of the future. We had quite the diverse amount of movies, music, and worldwide events. Computers were now surging forward with the release of Apple as well, and many artists were still making their statements through their music. Some being labeled controversial like Madonna's *'Like a Virgin'* whilst others were sending different messages teaching us about famine and poverty.

On November 25th, 1984, when a group of well-known musicians walked into a recording studio in Notting hill, London, magic was born with the making of *'Do they know it's Christmas?'*. A singer called Bob Geldof headed the group of artists naming themselves Band aid, with the song becoming a number one hit around the world, with all proceeds going to charity to support the Famine situation in Ethiopia. By 1984, famine in Ethiopia had already killed a million people. This song really opened our eyes to how horrific the situation was; it undoubtedly brought awareness to the world of how others were living, awareness we had no clue about, and these extreme poverty conditions brought sadness and confusion to many. We were a world that was advancing forward in leaps and bounds such as technology and the like, yet third world countries still existed, what was happening with our world. These conditions signified again that power and greed possess the world, and not love. For artists to use their power in such a way was inspirational to many, and hopeful that love and compassion could overcome devastation.

On the movie front so far in the '80s one of my favorite movies to hit our screen was *Footloose* – music, dance, and lots of little messages that were quite significant. Those that look at the pretty pictures and hum the tunes may not have found it touched their hearts in a deeper way of awareness, or the message it's sending, but for me, I learnt a lot through music and movies and could see that artists were making the biggest impact on society. Movies like *Sixteen Candles* and *The breakfast Club* were iconic also with messages for youth; our generation was experiencing such new territory in all areas, shown through the eyes of others. The Aids epidemic was still going strong with much discrimination and fear. Countries were still fighting or boycotting events which was always the case, but somehow the '80s so far had brought many great things that helped us to feel positive about change.

I was actually enjoying the 'all things matching' with fashions of the '80s and the way they focused on color. We had baggy tops tucked into high-waisted jeans with turned up cuffs and white socks, hair scarfs, permed hairdos, long dangly beaded necklaces, and button earrings. We wore short ruffled skirts, cropped tops, floral leggings, and legwarmers. Somewhere in there, those famous shoulder pads from decades earlier made a comeback. Guys grew their hair longer which looked great, and they wore lots of color – even pink, and the good thing was they really enjoyed it, they loved color and designs, and it looked good on them, it was uplifting and they looked happy…color brought more into their world. It was a decade of big hair, big jewelry, lots of denim, color, and court shoes. I loved the fashion, music, movies, and the diversity it formed. Most of us loved the '80s culture; it had a fun party element to it whilst we were trying to navigate ourselves through life.

Chapter 18
18. Single. Free

As the sun rose, I bounced out of bed happy as today was the day I would have my full independence. It was my *birthday* – not just any old birthday but I was 18 and able to acquire my driver's license. The only little problem was that should I obtain my license today; I still didn't have a car to drive. I had bought a little Mini, no idea why, again not sure where my brain was the last 12 months, but it looked cute at the time, and I liked cute things. It would be cheap on fuel and everyone told me it would be easy to drive. I'm not sure why they told me that, or how much faith my family and friends had in me driving, because I had excelled at my lessons. However, I blew them all away when I passed my driver's test with 98% and the only reason I lost 2% was because the policeman was in a hurry to return to the station and thought I was going too slow. Yes, that's the truth, he told my father to his face! It went a bit like this:

"I couldn't give her a perfect score, I had to take at least something off, so I took 2% off for that," was his reasoning.

Okay then, what was it about people not giving me the perfect score or acknowledgment I deserved, a trait that carried on through my life. So as excited as I was for my independence, I didn't quite have it yet because the mini wasn't ready, it was being spray painted by my boyfriend (that was his trade) to – you guessed it – pink. It also needed some mechanical work finished, so why did I buy a car that wasn't ready to drive, no idea, as I said, not sure where my head was when I bought it. But it was a letdown after finally securing my own independence, to not have a car to drive.

The day progressed and that night I was having my 18th birthday party in my parent's backyard. Family and friends came, I didn't really want a 'big bash', as I don't like lots of people around and preferred a smaller gathering. Recapping on my night, I can't really recall much as I was drinking, although, I wasn't really a drinker (as in to get paralytic drunk); but for the first time in my life, I had such mixed emotions about my future. Turning 18 jolted me to some revelations, and because of that I realized I had to change my life.

I still longed for that love, the ultimate 'The One' love, and I started to think we can never truly find what we are looking for if we don't break away from what we have, or who we have it with.

If we don't close one door, then another can't open

My boyfriend and I were very different; he wanted to marry, have children, and build a house, wanting a simple settled life. He didn't want to travel, backpack or even care if he went out of town, where as I did (as we know). When we became engaged so young it seemed like a good idea at the time, but it wasn't true love, it was a bit like 'maybe we should get married we have been dating for a while now' and so we did. This is not a reason to decide to spend the rest of your life with a person, and so the time had arrived.

I had dreams; I wanted to chase in life and those were first and foremost in my heart. Finding 'my one' that I'd felt all my life. However, I was a person that liked to please others and keep the peace, so it was going to be a rather large step for me to not only call off the engagement, but to cancel the wedding plans, as we had already made some bookings. As I sat each day weighing up my options, I knew I needed to choose myself. I deserved to be happy.

I confided in my father, who immediately discussed the importance of my happiness and choosing for me. He told me:

"Kell, you have to be happy, you must choose for you not anyone else and not worry what anyone else is going to think or say, you don't need anyone's approval – it's your life, not theirs, you are not here to please people – including your parents – you must follow your OWN heart and choose what

YOU want, what YOU love, what YOU desire in life. Choose for yourself."

At that point, we both expressed relief as I thought I would disappoint my parents with my choice to follow my heart and call off my engagement; but at the same time, they were relieved because they could see I wasn't following my heart. They could feel my energy and knew I wasn't really happy or living from my heart.

I learnt that day that your parents have such unconditional love for you and want to see you happy, they want you to be with the person that your heart beats for, the right person, and they want you to be free to choose in life what you desire. They don't want to see you settling, and they don't judge, they just want to see their child happy. My dad expressed relief as he could see it, and he could also see I was feeling pressured. He also, in that moment, told me he thought I was too young to get married. He said to me:

"Kellie, the choices we make at 14 are going to be different to what we choose for ourselves at 18."

My parents had been so supportive throughout my life and this was no exception, they had not expressed their concern earlier as they didn't want to interfere, but I was incredibly relieved when they showed me their understanding.

The wedding was cancelled, and although it hurt others around me, it was a decision I had to make for myself. Your life is too important to live it out of fear or on other people's terms, it's too important to not be living from love, a love that makes you feel truly, deeply, madly, in love. It's too important to waste time settling and staying in an okay or unfulfilling relationship if you're not happy. Life is fleeting – and if we are not careful, before we know it, we find years have passed, with us living each day the groundhog day of yesterday, then one day when it's too late, we wake up and see how it's all passed us by and we have lost, or not found, the very thing we came here to find – Love. I know this wasn't my case yet – but I wasn't about to allow myself to be a statistic, I would live my life and what I am here for.

At this time, another male had entered my life, possibly waking me to these feelings too and the knowing that I wasn't following my heart. It made me realize that I wasn't ready for any relationship, but ready to free myself and find who I really was.

***

Now that I was free, I started to plan my overseas adventure, I had saved well, sold my land that I shared with my ex-boyfriend, and felt free to pursue my dreams. EUROPE here I come.

Throughout this whole challenging process, my energy friend never appeared strongly, but there was a knowing I was being guided. I found the strength I needed in myself, so although, I couldn't feel him much, there was this inner soul presence pushing me to choose myself. It felt like he was getting me prepared for adulthood, and then hoping I could walk my own path strong and independent within myself, knowing who I was. It was a very interesting feeling.

As months passed by, it turned out I was definitely being guided. I found love with my future husband before I had time to pack my bags for my travel expedition, so needless to say my bags never got packed. You know how I've been saying when one door closes, it's so another can open? Well that was surely the case here. Something I had known for some time deep in my heart. I thought I would be torn between my much loved desire to travel and new found single independence, but it was to be the deepest love I'd discovered to this point, and as much as I tried to restrain myself, it felt completely and utterly right.

In light of this, though, I needed to take a few months for myself, to figure out what I really wanted even though every thought, every feeling came back to this man, and deep feelings were already there. We did have some kind of connection. It wasn't like my energy friend, but I could feel maybe he was my soulmate. I had met him and been around him earlier because he was my brother's friend, so we had been friends for quite some time, and he had spent time at our house on several occasions. We even worked together for a while, but all my attention had been on another. It wasn't until I was going through my growth stage of trying to really find who I was that something shifted in me, and I saw this man in a completely different light. When I shared my new found level of love for him, surprisingly, he felt the same, and we knew there was no turning back. He had watched me from afar knowing one day we would be together, he had said it was just an undeniable feeling and knowing we would, and he would wait as long as it took. We had common interests, similar ideas about life; he loved to travel and have adventures like me and was different to my previous boyfriend. A little more of a rebel, I would say. He had a bit of a reputation for being a ladies man, liked to have a drink or six as all young men his age, he was very athletic, played tennis, and had big dreams.

We started dating and pretty quickly we moved in together. I had moved out of my parent's home a while ago and was renting a house with a friend, he was there most nights, and we just both knew it felt right for him to move in. It all happened fast, but we just knew. As life moved forward, I felt for the first time I was on track, aligned with where I was supposed to be. I still had no clue what I was supposed to be doing for work. I was back working in Real Estate after hurting my lower back in a previous employment whilst being up a ladder. I had almost fallen from the ladder while I was juggling a heavy box and trying to stop myself from falling; I damaged my lower discs and couldn't work in that field any more. But for now, I was content to be where I was and see what the universe guided. Yes, I still let the universe (or my energy friend more to the point) guide me as I always did, and most times these days I not only paid attention, I actually did make my choices from that guidance. *I know – I was finally learning – not before time!*

A group of us *yet again* decided to take another overseas trip. Where to this time? It was getting exciting choosing our next destination. We chose a place we were all keen for and one that was starting to really make an impression with Aussies. So we booked, and not long after it was *time for travel!* And I was excited to be traveling with my new partner for our first adventure together.

Chapter 19
BALI

Flying out of Melbourne on the 'Red Kangaroo' there were ten of us this time journeying – My brother, cousins, partners, and friends – heading for some adventures in the sun. Shortly after consuming the usual 'chicken or beef' a drink or three and watching a movie, we touched down in Denpasar for our first experience of this Hindu island they call Bali.

Bali in the early '80s was just amazing; it was an undeveloped paradise sanctuary popular for surfers, hippies, spirituality and was on most young people's list to visit. Momentum was building with the Aussies that Bali was the place to be. It was known for many things, including 'surfer's heaven', with some of the best breaks in the world coming out of Uluwatu. It was inexpensive and laid back.

Our drive from the airport into town surprised us with much lack in surroundings but such richness in culture. It was a very new experience for us, and perhaps, one would say a 'culture shock' but before long we came to our first stop which was Kuta Beach. Kuta demonstrated unmade roads, very few hotels, and lots of backpacker's accommodation; however, we decided we would live it up a little and booked into the epic 'Ocean Blue Club Resort'. We soon learnt the ways of Bali and how to get around, if you didn't feel like walking, you rented a car, bike, or scooter, and when we wanted to travel as a group, we would take a Bemo to usher us around the island from place to place, all very inexpensive.

A few days in, we decided to hire a car which turned out to be a bright-orange, funky Jeep for the few of us that didn't want to try our hand at motor cycles, (which was me) and for the others that wanted the experience. They took their life into their hands and followed behind. It was a little hairy on the roads because we discovered road rules were not top priority in Bali, and as we approached any intersection our hearts started racing not knowing who was going first. Everyone just put their foot on the accelerator and hoped for the best, it was first in first serve pretty much, no one really knew who had the right of way, no lights or signals, but we were blown away at how it flowed so well and there were little accidents.

Kuta consisted of one 'main' strip and 'of course' let's not forget the famous 'Poppy's Lane'. Upon investigating the shopping situation early on because I couldn't wait to see what was around, we discovered some fairly rough and ready market stalls along with some 'open shed' tin shops on the side of the road. This was nothing like we had ever seen; we loved the vibe it oozed and thought all our Christmases had come at once when we discovered massages for what seemed like 20 cents. *(Maybe a slight exaggeration there but you get my drift.)* At this point in Bali, it wasn't commercialized which meant it wasn't overridden with nightclubs and alcohol. There was alcohol, there were nightclubs, but let it be known none of this was out of control. Peanuts nightclub was a popular club on the entertainment strip that we enjoyed, but in these times, it was all a lot more fun, innocent, and laid back. Magic Mushies were on the menu in some places, however, I never tried, it wasn't really my thing plus I, certainly, didn't need anything else to make me feel like I was in another world, I was already doing okay with that myself. I kind of felt like I floated through Bali, although, I couldn't feel him he must have been with me because I felt that undeniable protection in every way. Being in a foreign country – and let's face it for the first time arriving in Bali – it was an experience compared to Australia. But so far, we loved it.

We stayed in traditional authentic rooms surrounded by lush tropical gardens, a swimming pool, and everyone made friends with the interesting little creatures called Geckos walking up your walls. These days in Bali it was cool down by the breeze of the overhead fans, no air conditioners, but I loved the primitive lifestyle. It was a place that exuded peace, emanated harmony, and radiated love. As we sat around the pool taking it all in, sipping drinks in this divine setting, we were all enjoying such a chilled atmosphere, listening to music, chatting and sharing.

Shopping I was a tad excited about because everything was so cheap (so it's fair to say we did a bit of that, just a bit) cassette tapes, t-shirts, singlets, and sarongs, the clothes didn't last long but they were so cheap it didn't matter. Slogans like 'Been there done that' and 'I've been to Bali too' were popular. The beaches were beautiful and palm trees lined the coast. There were no hotels on the beach at this point to block your views or become overrun by tourists, so you could hear the waves splashing from your hotel, it was so peaceful. Balinese people were incredibly friendly and the food was delicious. What's not to like! We were so surprised how the Balinese would bend over backwards to accommodate in any way, they are such beautiful, kind people and nothing was a problem.

One morning, we decided to take in the sights out of Kuta, so we all decided lets go up to Ubud in the mountains to explore and visit the monkey forest, it sounded like a good idea. We were really keen to explore this wonderful island as much as possible. The little village of Ubud oozed spiritual energy, ancient temples, and traditional culture. It was for those that wanted to get away from it all in an even more tranquil setting, and be guided by the energies and surrounds of a 'ZEN' lifestyle. You could practice yoga, meditation with the sounds of the forest so silent and calming. I fell in love with Ubud and wished we had added a few nights in our itinerary to stay. There were many sacred places hidden from view off the main road that caused you to go searching, a day definitely wasn't long enough I could have stayed there a week. It was just so beautiful.

As we were returning driving through the country side to visit some villages, we were stunned at the first sight of their gorgeous green rice fields that appeared to go on for miles. We wanted to stop at an authentic local village to meet the people. Upon approaching the village and stepping out of the vehicle, everyone came up to us – so welcoming and grateful. We saw that the smallest purchase lit up their faces with a smile that would warm anyone's heart. They had very little. It was living in poverty to us; I was shocked at how others in our world lived. They worked so hard day and night to accommodate their families as best they could just to be living in such poor conditions. As I looked around at these people, the one thing that took me back was, for having so little they appeared so content, they were happy. They knew of no different, they had no idea of our world, well most didn't, not in the villages anyway, but yet life to them was so simple. In a way, I was envious but in another felt so privileged. Why is it that some of us are born into riches in lands where we have access to everything and yet others into these conditions. It didn't seem fair, such a significant difference. We appeared to be living on different planets because I couldn't fathom the amount of people here and around the world that lived in such third world conditions. Although they seemed happy, I felt sad for what I saw.

Buying a handmade leather bracelet or necklace didn't feel enough to me, I just wanted to hand over all my money to these beautiful kind people. I couldn't give enough, and when we left the ones out in the more 'discreet areas', I wondered how many times they see tourists pass by and how much they would sell. As much as I was having an amazing time, I felt like I wanted to take them all back to Melbourne with me, but of course we couldn't do that, and I did realize they are accustomed to how they live. They didn't know any different and who's to say they would want to live our way of life anyway, I certainly had my doubts at times. Overall, it was such an authentic 'eye opening' experience.

Back in Kuta – as I shopped, I was drawn more to explore side streets with markets and places where I could see they needed my purchase more than others. Supporting the few glamorous shops wasn't on my list, I'm sure it was easier and quicker to reach, but I wanted to help as much as I could. Often I got lost, as my navigational skills completely suck. Wherever I go, I don't seem to concentrate on how I get there and find that I have absolutely no idea how to get back. The others learnt earlier that if I was going shopping, than someone really should come with me, that way I didn't get lost or go missing for hours. Most times, I went with my new man, and he was quite content to allow me to shop away whilst he watched or made his few purchases. I'm sure you have realized by now I did like to shop, it was all so new to me, I loved all the hippie stuff.

However, most of the boys liked to consume alcohol pretty regularly and as shopping for them adds up to a couple of singlets and a T-shirt, we didn't see them out in the markets much. (Unless they were buying music tapes.)

Many hours were spent with lazy days around the pool, drinks in hand with tunes playing, nothing was a rush in Bali and everything went pretty slow and simple. We felt we were living like kings and queens with everything at our fingertips at so very little cost, Australia was so expensive compared to Bali. We had never experienced anything like it; it was like a dream come true for us.

Keeping to our task of trying to explore as much as we could, we decided a trip out to one of the local nearby islands would be fun. In true Bali fashion, we discovered just how *chilled* they were. As we boarded this small dinghy boat, very simple nothing flash, we left the shore to travel out to the island, however, noticed fairly early that it was leaking. Water was spurting up from the middle of the boat flowing out onto our feet. (We didn't realize when we booked the trip it came with lessons on how to scoop water out of the leaking dinghy with supplied ice-cream containers.) As we brought it to the attention of the Balinese driver he smiled and said:

"Oh, yes, it leaks, it's no problem, use container please scoop out water for me it only small leak."

So my vision of my brother in his bright blue shorts shoveling out water from our boat, so we didn't sink was one we all couldn't forget. Everything was just 'not a problem' in Bali, and he so casually knew the boat had a leak but we wouldn't sink so 'no problem'.

We made it to the island and back again all was *'no problem',* and we all learned just why these beautiful race of people lived fairly stress free! Nothing was a problem!

Zinc Cream, sunglasses, swimsuits, and hair braids (all girls got them) sunsets, cocktails, and massages, lots of fun in the sun. Australians had discovered Bali's blissed out state and their laid back harmonious culture, their soul sacred traditions created such a peaceful ambiance and energy, and it became the favorite place to visit so close to our shores. It was just taking off with the tourist scene, but I was so grateful I got to experience it whilst so young and Bali so raw, to see the authentic beautiful Bali before the onslaught of development was an absolute treasure.

As I write this I still hear the Australian band Redgum singing their hit song 'I've been to Bali too'. It often hums in my head – it was a fun Aussie song that become a hit with everyone, depicting exactly just how relaxed a trip to this island was

After two weeks of this incredible experience, sadly, it was time to board our Qantas flight back home. The adventure was over, and all I could think was how do I get to live here for a while. I felt so drawn to Bali in every way and didn't want to leave, there were Australians that lived there, backpackers on long visas, surfers that didn't go home. I desired to stay, live amongst this laid-back hippie lifestyle, I wasn't keen to return to our way of living, and I would have loved a break for a while. My new partner loved the warm weather like me, he liked surfing, water sports, and tropical islands so he didn't object. Bali was so cheap to live, and we didn't need to work but we didn't think we could follow our hearts and try it out, not many were brave enough to really. We had to go back home, but I knew one day I would return.

Chapter 20
Connections

After Bali, life moved along in many different ways, and my relaxed existence, of how I knew it, was slipping away. Do you ever notice how the responsibilities of adulthood continue to push us to our limits, more each year than the one before? Before we know it – it becomes a relentless cycle of keeping up with all around us. Often this causes us to slide deeper into fears, money worries, working longer hours, keeping up with a mortgage, bills and so on. My life was no different as I succumbed to this way of living within this paradigm...*and I had absolutely no idea why or what I was thinking.*

I started my life with my new partner which had seen us married within 16 months. It was rather quick and came out of the blue for me, but we both knew it was right, and when you know you just know. In some way, I knew it was my contract, don't ask me how, I just knew, and for that reason. I gave it all I had. We were very happy (until we weren't) but the years we spent together through all of our triumphs and tragedies we shared a beautiful time and one that had us both remain well respected by the other.

Although I was in love with him, with who I felt was my 'soulmate', I knew the love was still different to what I had experienced, that love that had eluded me in the physical form to date. However, the love I experienced with my husband seemed to be the closest to that love I had known, and for that I was most grateful to God, the universe, the power above, for sending me a man along with love for me to share and experience throughout my journey.

My missing piece that was absent throughout my life remained, and as I sunk deeper into the world of the matrix and materialism, the void became even greater. When I married my husband, I think in my mind I gave up ever thinking my beautiful love, him, would ever join me in this life, and because of that I feel I may have hid him further.

I felt he was still walking with me, though, and in some way it was like he was guiding me to a better life. I didn't *feel* him so much anymore but things would just happen out of the blue. I would ask for help in ways to handle situations, emotions, and I was shown. I was a long way from that little girl now, but I still felt lost, that feeling never went away, and I guess as long as you still feel like you're missing half of you that feeling never would. The few times I felt him now I flowed with it always, as he blissfully streamed in and out, and as my 'awareness' allowed the deeper and stronger connection, I could sometimes feel him more. *In so many ways, he had carried me in his arms through this thing we call life on earth, and I knew in a way he was still doing it.*

I had not heard his voice since I was 16, telling me I must stay as I was here for something important, that was all the information I received, and right at this moment, it felt like a lifetime ago – *I missed him so deeply.*

Still knowing I was here to do something important, but no clue as to what direction to look for that, I wondered would I do it now. Or was I supposed to do it later in life? If it was now, it had better get a wriggle on.

Living from masks had taken its toll on me, and I was a fairly nervous person by now. I didn't like crowds or many people around, that hadn't changed, but I thought if I'm to find what it is I'm meant to do in this life I have to put myself out there, so I did, very reluctantly.

I signed with an agency for acting, TV, and modelling work thinking this may be the path to being found or doing my purpose, but with no acting experience I was mostly stuck with extra roles being up against many experienced actors. So that didn't work. I didn't have much faith in the universe at this stage, because after years of calling in my beautiful friend to be with me, he was still in energy form, not with me, so someone wasn't '*really*' listening to my requests.

Each day I had traveled, my whole life to date, there was nothing or no one that quite fit like 'him'. He was 'the one', 'my one', a part of me. I had tried to find him here in my world, but hadn't as yet, I knew if he appeared I would know him immediately, but I wondered in a way, had I given up?

In saying that, sometimes in the early days of my marriage I would feel his energy, and I would still turn around thinking someone was there, thinking he will appear, looking over my shoulder, like I used too, the presence was so strong at certain times. It was like he was there, so powerful. And in those times I started to open to him again, and the more I did the stronger the connection and more pure the love became, but keeping it open was difficult for me, because it felt like he was staying away, and the more I tried the harder he felt to reach, but perhaps that was because my world had changed considerably.

The thing with being human, though, is we are here to experience the 'physical', we are designed to desire touch, feel, emotion, intimacy, sex, embracing…all those can only come from another physical being. So as much as I yearned for this undeniable euphoric love, it wasn't here for me to reach out and touch in a physical body. I made a choice one day that I possibly had to let him go and try to not feel him, to carry on with my life. How I would ever do this I had no idea. He has walked with me for just over 20 years, and I knew a large part of me, myself, was always going to be lost without him, I wasn't sure if he would ever fully go away because if he was in me, part of me, then of course he couldn't, but I was clueless to what our connected love and energy truly was.

My husband and I started to pave out our life together, we had built a home the year we got married and moved in shortly after. We were both now in the world of 'DINKS' (Double income no kids) and both working six days a week. Everything seemed to be cruising along fine until I had another altercation at my employment with sexual harassment. Back in Real Estate again (not sure what it was with real estate), however, one of the salesman decided he might like a bit of a grab and touch for his own pleasure whenever he choose, without seeming to ask my permission first, or passing me the memo. What was it about these men? They all had wives and no respect for women. I was in my early twenties now and a long way from

171

that 16-year-old girl that was scared half to death and being mortified to tell anyone. This time I reported him immediately, but the manager along with the others in the office all acted like it was a bit of a joke, along with the opinion it was fully acceptable. They only made me feel more degraded and disrespected. I was in an office of males this time that had absolutely no concern for me. Again, what was wrong with these men? They acted all righteous like it was nothing. I stayed on for a little while hoping my voice was heard, but after several more altercations, it was clear he was not going to stop attacking me from behind. I hadn't shared with my husband at this point, as he would have knocked the guy out and ended up getting arrested, which I didn't want. But the time had come for me to leave. I told my husband and resigned immediately.

It was approaching summer, so as the timing fit perfectly, I decided I would take the summer off to enjoy and scout for a job afterwards. That didn't really last long, as three weeks into my lovely holiday I stepped in to help my brother in his business. He owned his own travel agency but his business partner had to take a long absence through a personal matter leaving him short staffed. I stepped into the world of travel, what was to be a temporary situation, and never left. My days in travel were born – for many years to come. It was obviously the universe aligning my job situation again, fitting quite perfectly and for that I was grateful. I could see travel was where I was meant to be and working in a family business.

My husband seemed to know how it felt to not follow your purpose, he had a missing piece of his own and a path he knew was his to take in this life. As a young boy, he showed extreme talents to become a professional tennis player. He was selected and asked to be taken away from his home town to train to become a professional world athlete on the tennis circuit. He had the skills to be at the top, and he knew it. He was left handed and belted down those serves already as fast as most professional players on the circuit. However, through circumstances he never left to pursue his dream, and because of that his dream had slipped away. He continued to play, but I could see the regrets had started to eat away at him.

Not long after marrying, we were having a discussion around this topic one night, and he mentioned how he could have gone on to be a professional coach, as some of the players he had beaten years earlier were coaching world class professional tennis athletes, he remarked how that could be him. I took it all in, listening, watching, and as he spoke I could see the hurt and regret he felt. The next day, I sat him down and offered for him to go and do it, that it wasn't too late, that I would travel the circuit with him and he could work his way up to coaching the elite. He knew he could do it, he knew he could make it, and he thought about it for a while, but after sometime, he decided he had 'missed the opportunity' and his life was here and now. I would have happily packed up, sold our home, and traveled around the world with him to have this opportunity. I wanted him to live his dream, at least one of us knew what we were here for, so why not try it, and if it didn't work, we could always return to our life here. After many attempts to get him to change his mind, he declined lovingly with gratitude after deciding he felt that ship had sailed.

I felt for him because if anyone knew how he felt it was me. It made me see there were two of us in this marriage that had a knowing of something greater, not that we weren't happy with each other, we truly were in love, but we both seemed to have a loss.

When I stepped into this marriage, it not only came with my husband but with his loving family as well. He was from a family of boys with a mother that had yearned for a daughter; so needless to say, she felt she finally had her daughter. They were very loving and their generosity and kindness towards me was instant in every way, welcoming me into their family and treating me like one of their own. It made life easier to be able to get along with your in-laws, and I considered myself very fortunate. I had not only gained a husband and loving in-laws but two other brothers as well. I could never strike it for a sister! – not that I was complaining – but I seemed to always have boys around me growing up.

Our life started to take a turn more towards the materialistic world rather than the world or lifestyle I had grown up with. It had become more about money, designer labels, owning a house, mortgage, and when are you starting a family. It was a far cry who I was or where I had come from, none of these things I ever thought would rule my life, but somehow I only had myself to blame for implementing them to this point. As my stress levels grew, so did my ability to cope, and I had a mini stroke. As minor as it was, I knew the universe was sending me a message, I was far too far off my path and this was a little warning to slow down and find myself. It was to be one of my many wake-up calls.

Society conditioning tells us at certain ages we should have already achieved 'things'. It goes a little like this:

So now your 18, you're an adult, and you need to be responsible, now your 21 you should be thinking about buying your own home, oh now you're married when are you having children, and now you've had one baby when is the next coming, and so on it goes! Not once does anyone stop to think that we might not all want to live like sheep and follow the norm, maybe some don't want to get married, or buy a house or have children. No one ever asks you if you're living your dream, living from your heart, happy, or enjoying life. People just seem to follow on like sheep, and I never imagined myself as part of the flock.

***

The '80s

...was ending and closing out as one of the most influential decades of all time. A decade that would definitely go down in history books as one of the most remembered of all, and by all of us that traveled from puberty through to adulthood, us teens that grew up in the '80s as our era...***this is how we saw it.***

I have already mentioned some but here's a lot more...big hair, shoulder pads, mini-skirts and leg warmers, pastels, neon, black and white with denim, pointy shoes, pink 'lots of pink' and hair scrunchies. (Don't, let's forget about those.) We had hilarious sitcoms that made you laugh so hard your stomach hurt and controversial music that always kept it interesting. The Titanic was found (finally – it only took them 73 years), and the Berlin Wall came down, whilst the multi-colored cube that got everyone thinking was invented. (I loved that cube.) We had Pacman, Band Aid, and CD's, Johnny Depp, and Jump Street.

'INXS', 'Midnight Oil', 'Men At Work' – were all 'Aussie bands', showing the world how it's done in the land 'Down Under' and we were most extremely proud! We had Nintendo's video games, *'Donkey Kong'* and *'Frogger'* (my favorites). We started the space shuttle era that became no longer, and by the end of the '80s, PCs had erupted within the homes of many that were deemed 'lucky' enough to afford one.

...and for some more in the world of music and movies.

Michael Jackson was bringing awareness to 'heal the world' with his music, light and love, which the world certainly needed. He had also stepped up along with Lionel Richie and Quincey Jones (shortly after Band Aid recorded their single *'Do they know it's Christmas'*) to bring USA artists together recording a song called *'We are the world'* as a charity song, also for African famine relief. From here came more charities, and it appeared the '80s were kicking it on a mission to save the world. Michael Jackson and his music went on to make an impression around the world about love and peace, showing us we were all here together to join as one united nation on our planet.

A young and upcoming actor slid across the floor in his underwear, engaged with a prostitute when his parents were out of town, and consequently turned the house into a brothel. (I mean, seriously, who didn't want to see Tom Cruise in his underwear.)

A religious town made it illegal to dance and listen to rock music (I wouldn't have survived there). A young newcomer decided this was ridiculous, because dance is a form of expression and everybody should be given the privilege to express themselves through dance, so he fought to overturn this law and won.

Another new actor took us back to the future in a sci-fi classic with his eccentric 'Einstein' look alike friend 'the Doc'.

Finally an alien came to talk to us whilst all the time wanting to fly home, and I learnt a few karate moves whilst strangely adapting a bond, *for some reason* to the *'Karate Kid'* movies.

Apart from all else, romantic movies along with dance movies were still my favorites. *'Fame'* showed us not only how hard it was to cut it in a dance school, but some important life lessons, and *'Flashdance'* brought the attention of not only her incredible dance skills to the forefront, but the fact a woman could be a welder working alongside men in this world. I didn't really understand the full extent of feminism, but this surprised me and stood out as a huge leap in society for me.

'The breakfast club' was an iconic timeless classic, sensationally displaying to us how to 'accept each other' that it's absolutely okay to be 'who we are' and not judge 'anyone'. It showed us in a pivotal moment that we are all wearing masks to fit in, trying to be someone else, someone others want us to be, amidst the yearning and desire to be ourselves. More importantly it sent a message to the individual to accept yourself *first* for who you are, then you would not need to fear what others thought of you, there would not be a need to *try* to fit in, we would simply just be *us* without the fear of being *us*.

The movie sent a very important message to not only us youth at that time, but to the collective, for if we all took a little more notice of the real hidden message here and actually integrated it into our lives, how might this world be? I'm not sure how many understood the bigger message in this movie. (I know I didn't at the time) But it did help influence future society by touching on themes such as disconnection, bullying, judgment, and stereotyping.

Being a movie girl, I have to mention we had some of the best ever movies made in the '80s. *Top Gun, Risky Business, Footloose, Fame, Flashdance, Endless Love, The Breakfast Club, Back to the Future, Karate Kid, ET, An Officer and a Gentlemen, Indiana Jones, Dirty Dancing, Pretty in Pink, Die Hard, Dead Poets Society, Ghost Busters, Ferris Bueller, Sixteen Candles, The Terminator, Aliens, First Blood,* and *Summer Lovers.* Still to this day, we are shown messages within movies, music, lyrics, books, and universal signs in everyday life, and although these messages are spreading wide and far, there are still many that don't pay attention.

I loved our era with the absence of mobile devices, texting, and social media, it meant we talked face to face; we couldn't hide behind a screen. As hard as it was to face ourselves and others sometimes it was inescapable, at some point we just had to. This upheld connection within relationships to others more so than today. Today's world of modern technology does elude our youth from this opportunity, thus, remaining deeper in the emotional state depicted to us by social status.

***

Chapter 21
No Goodbyes

The time had come, where had he gone? I got so used to him traveling with me through life, he now had disappeared. There had been no sign of him for a while. I tried to reconnect several times but nothing, he had vanished. He had not said goodbye, or told me he was leaving me. It surprised me because I had always been able to connect at some point, or at least feel him surge in and out, but nothing. And I wondered why he would leave me without saying goodbye. It didn't seem like it was something he would do, I thought for sure he would tell me if he was leaving, unless of course there was a reason he couldn't. I thought he would be around forever, and that one day my dream might actually come true. Maybe that was silly thinking on my part, the little girl that dreamed of her perfect love standing in front of her, but alas she had still dreamed. Even when she had grown older and become an adult, she still dreamed of the one thing she prayed for each night when younger, asking the universe and her energy love to come and be with her. She had never stopped secretly asking or hoping. She had faith.

I was hurting; I couldn't believe he was gone. I had a lifetime of incredible memories and feelings of us walking together, and even knowing that when I couldn't feel him he was there, all I had to do was connect in, but this time was different. He appeared to be gone.

I wish I knew why he left, or if I was the reason he left. I couldn't see why because we had my lifetime together to date, and his love for me would not just change. The years we spent, he just wouldn't forget them, the laughs, fun, togetherness since I was three years old, or maybe even earlier, I know that meant everything to him to. I know he wouldn't just leave me without an explanation, he wouldn't. But I was now walking alone.

I thanked the universe for allowing him to share himself, his energy and the most profound love of existence with me; I thanked him for loving me unconditionally in this way, with such pure euphoric infinite love, and for always being with me. I thanked him for his incredible protection of me, guidance, support, and how he never let me down. I thanked him for saving my life, not just once, but many times when I thought about it, he was my beacon of light and together I felt like we both shone. We had something so special, beyond words. Something I possibly could never put into words. Intuitively though, I knew somehow we were still connected but I wasn't sure I would ever feel him again. I hoped he could hear me extending my love to him, how honored I felt and my gratitude, and I hoped he would feel just how incredibly sacred he was to me. I hoped he could hear me, because I never got to say goodbye.

Sometimes in life, we don't know what we've got until it's gone. I wished I had not hid him and myself throughout my life from a seven-year-old, if only I didn't. I wished I had the courage to be myself. To show our love and share what we had together, because that was very much a privilege. I felt like I had let him down, let us down, and that I hadn't showed him just how incredibly deep I loved him, and how deeply honored I was. I felt I had not brought us together in the way I was meant to, deep inside I always thought I would one day, when I was ready, but I guess now my chance had gone. I had long enough, but now I didn't have that chance anymore. I had waited too long, and now he had gone.

Chapter 22
Life

As I now was traveling alone, I started to feel myself fall deeper into the world of social beliefs. I was suffering some depression since my energy love had left, and I just couldn't find the enthusiasm to keep going. I knew he would want me to keep going, and I had to do it for him, after all he carried me through so far, and I wondered what it was I was still meant to do, because nothing was showing up in my world, in fact, I felt my purpose was getting buried deeper. I was aware I had to be careful after my minor health scare, and I tried not to stress. But I didn't really belong in this structured belief system.

Social Culture and Systems: *"A set of beliefs, customs, practices and behaviors that exists within a population."*

I would have liked to tell people what they could do with their social culture. Yes, that about sums it up, and that's how I felt. I saw firsthand for the first time so intricately how social class was defined, the levels of acceptance and importance. This wasn't the first time I had seen this reality, but now as an adult it was pushed in my face somewhat more, and who the hell wanted to live like this!

Do you own a home or do you rent? Do you drive a new car or an old one? Do you work collar and tie or a trade? Do you have diamonds on your fingers or zirconia's? Do you wear brand names or no names?

I saw the pressure people were under to conform, all to avoid being identified as a lower class. The burden of carrying out the task to become the social status they desired. Did we tick all the boxes? Was it all for show? I'm sure people asked themselves this daily. More so they underwent continual stress and workloads to be able to tick the right boxes. What had people become? Lives were focused towards working only to spend money on materialistic needs not required but desired, not needed but to keep a status. *Was there anything left over to enjoy life?* I think I had reluctantly joined the masses, sad to say. I'm not sure that I saw much love around but there was a whole lot of judgment and fear.

Throughout my twenties, I had gone through what seemed like enough family deaths to last me a lifetime, and to be honest, I wondered when it would stop. It got to the point where I couldn't go a year without losing someone. Some were not as close to me as others but it was still a difficult time, and constantly having deaths every year was too much.

Many years had passed since we were married, and we were still childless. We were now both working seven days a week, as we had purchased a convenience store that kept us living on the Peninsula. We had plans to move north interstate up on the east coast of Australia where the weather was nicer, but for some reason, we ended up buying this business and staying. It was all quite strange as I was ready to move away, I felt I had outgrown our small town having lived here all my life. My husband felt the same too and he was keen to move, but somehow we remained. We had been trying to have a child, but it was not working out so well for us, resulting in some heartbreaks and disappointments. We had been trying for years, and I was about to give up when I was guided to try one more time, and to our surprise, after all these years, I found out I was pregnant! So after years, we had endured traumas and deaths, we were elated when we discovered I was pregnant with our child, and it was a very happy time in our lives. We were both over the moon along with our families that had watched us go through everything over the years.

Intuitively, I knew it was a girl as soon as I found out, and I was correct. I didn't need a scan to tell me and we elected not to ask the doctor. However, a week before I delivered her I fell over some paving in a shopping village that was sticking up. As I fell, I tried to brace my tummy as not to damage my baby, but I was taken to hospital for a check-up just in case. Our baby was fine, I had protected her well the way I fell, but the nurse offered up the information that 'she' was doing fine, before she asked us if we knew what the sex of our baby was, of course I knew anyway but now I did know 100% for sure. A week later, I went into labor and after 20 hours she was born, she arrived two days after her due date but of course it was on a master number 11 and a very special day in astrology. I don't know why I was surprised; I don't think anything could surprise me by this stage. She entered this world and took my breath away, and as the nurse placed her on my stomach, and I heard those words from spirit, "This one's special, she is here to do something big," my first thought was, *oh no, here we go again?* As much as my ego wanted to say NO, I knew my guidance was correct.

The minute I found out I was pregnant, my intuition and psychic abilities returned, I was open, I could feel, hear, and see again. One thing I noticed though was I still couldn't feel 'him', as open as I was.

As I held my newborn baby in my arms, my heart was overjoyed, she was the most precious thing I had ever seen. Her eyes looking like they were looking up at me, she was so gorgeous I couldn't believe I finally had a baby girl – a child of my own. However, whilst this should have been the most incredible moment of my life, I was dealing with something internally that was breaking my heart. I was trying to not think about my adored father sitting in a different hospital having chemotherapy.

My world had collapsed two months prior to our daughter's birth when my dad was diagnosed with lung cancer, one of happiest times of my life would be overshadowed by the most tragic, once again not a fan of the universe at this point. All I kept thinking was how cruel, and why? Why now? I mean why at all, but couldn't you have picked your times a little better. I had waited for years to have a child and to be able to give my parents their first grandchild, so why now? I was upset not just for me but my father as well; he had waited so long and was so excited about his new grandchild. Now instead of enjoying 'with us', our new family addition and holding his new granddaughter in his arms; he was someplace else battling the fight of his life. I can only imagine how he must have been feeling, to be alone in that hospital whilst we were all celebrating the birth of our beloved Paris in my local hospital? Such an iconic time and he wasn't able to be there. My mum, of course, was there and my in-laws which did feel special. I was grateful, but my heart was bleeding for my father that he couldn't share this moment with me.

Chapter 23
Letting Go

Adjusting to parenthood, being a mother, was new, but my little girl lit up my world. She was a bright shining star and I was over the moon. But as I sat one afternoon with her in my arms, it dawned on me, as lucky as I felt, I realized that even miracles in my life like giving birth, having this gorgeous angel of a child in my arms, plus other magical moments I had experienced, all still had not filled my missing piece. Everything I had achieved or experienced in this physical life had not ever replaced that feeling that, something or someone was absent from me. In some way I had still waited for it to arrive in my life, but so far it had still escaped me.

Three months after my little girl was born, my father's cancer went into remission, and we were all so elated, we prayed it would not return and he would experience a full recovery but again, the universe had other ideas. As time moved on, my parents went on a holiday and over the next many months remained hopeful, enjoying life as much as they could together. But one month before my daughter's first birthday, we received the devastating news that my father's cancer had returned, and once again the tumor had grown rapidly and was considerably sizable. To my father, doctor's words were gospel and when his doctor looked him in the eye and said, "There is nothing more we can do," my father crashed. In other words, the doctor was saying, "Go home to die."

The mind is such a powerful tool, if you give into your thoughts, fears and your negative way of thinking you may as well give up before even trying. It took a lot of persuading and helping him to understand, that many cancer patients get that news but survive by way of being positive, using natural treatments and changing their diet, and above all else, staying out of fear

With months of natural treatments, new diet, along with an exceptional amount of study of treatments and cures to help my father, we were fighting a losing battle. Those treatments I talk about did, in fact, buy him seven more months after that doctor sent him home to die, with weeks to live. Those treatments did reduce and almost rid his massive tumor in that time, he shouldn't have still been here, and when my father died he didn't die of cancer, he died of complications. Which in his mind he had convinced himself he would…this is one of the last conversations we had.

Sitting in the chair, he looked up at me, those eyes starting to glaze over, sadness deep within, and the look on his face knowing the words he was about to speak would not only destroy me but he feared, would disappoint. I knew what was coming and every part of me wanted to shut down and run away.

"Kell, I don't want to live anymore. I'm tired, tired of it all, and if I have to live like this, I don't want to. I'm tired of living on juices and foods I don't like, I'm tired of not being able to eat red meat or drink a glass of beer, I'm tired of trying to get used to foods I have never seen in my life. I'm tired. I'm going to go anyway; I want to go how I want to go, just let me go."

"Dad, isn't living worth changing your diet, it seems a small price to pay for your survival, there is nothing wrong with healthy eating, vegetables, plant based foods free from toxins, it's a healthy way of living and you would get used to it. Please stay with us, don't give up, it will get better I promise. Stay with us. Stay for me, please, stay, I can't lose you."

As the tears rolled down his eyes, he looked into mine and spoke those dreaded words I will never forget:

"I'm so sorry, honey, I can't, I can't do it anymore, just let me go."

As he spoke tears were streaming down our faces, his as well as mine, and in that moment I knew I had lost him, my beautiful dad. What do you say to that? I begged him to stay, I begged him to try, to trust me that it would get better, it was only early days of the alternate treatments and we had sensational results. He struggled to regain his faith again after the doctor had told him he would die. Natural therapies and therapists, diet change, alternate medicines, all crushed his cancer within months of its return; however, those initial words rang deep in his mind.

Some believe doctor's words are gospel, some cling to the hope that they know everything, they are the closest to gods on this earth in some people's eyes. My father, well I don't know about the gods, but he sure did believe they knew everything, and that my alternate ways were no more than a fleeting practice to prolong, or not accept the obvious outcome. It didn't matter how many successful cases I researched and read to him, he gave up hope.

Nursing someone you love and watching them dying each day a little more in front of you is something I would never wish on my worst enemy. My father didn't want to be admitted to hospital so Mum and I granted him his last wishes and nursed him at home, where he was more comfortable, and where a nurse came daily to help. He wasn't in any pain, so he didn't need pain medication.

My beautiful father slipped away one night at 8:30 pm, only minutes after I left him to return to my home. As I kissed him goodbye and walked out the door, I knew it would be the last time I saw him, my spirit guides had told me, and it was. I was completely broken, I lost my rock, my mate, and felt like a part of my heart would be lost forever. A part of me left with him that night, and I knew I would never ever feel the same again.

My dad supported me in everything I ever attempted to do, or chose in my life, he never judged, not even for a moment. He showed me how to love unconditionally, to accept and allow others for who they are, to always show kindness and generosity to others. My parents had always both shown us they did not judge or try to control. They watched from the side lending support when necessary, but not interfering. I watched in wonder of many other parents around me growing up that were not like this, and I realized quite early how lucky I was, having these beautiful souls as my beloved parents.

My father lost his fight at 59, I was 29 and beyond devastated.

***

With the birth of my beautiful girl, she had brought with her so much love that filled our home, she also seemed to bring with her a full awareness of the spirit world (as I said here we go again! Like mother like daughter).

She had entered this world and was able to see and hear. From as early as being on the change table, she would look over my shoulder and be reaching out to someone giggling away like she was touching someone with her hand. It happened most days, and I knew from then on she had it all, just like me. As she grew, she would sit up in her bed chatting away to them, but there was no one viewed by our physical eyes in the room. She was always looking, gazing and smiling, giggling, pointing and chatting…and as I would stand there watching her I would ask her many times.

"Who are you talking to, love, who's there?" (Just like my mother did with me).

And Paris would respond: "My friend, Mummy, my friend."

After my father passed away, my mum moved in to live with us for a while. Watching her go through the loss of Dad was heartbreaking on top of what I was going through myself. I was devastated, and I found it hard to concentrate on anything in life, or get myself back on track. My mum was the same. I felt I had to be there for her though in any given moment, so in a way I suppressed more of my grief to be 'there' for mum when needed. The only thing that made this horrible ordeal bearable and put a smile on our face each day was our beautiful Paris. In some strange way, it felt like the universe had brought her in now to be able to help Mum and I at this traumatic time, having her first grandchild kept her busy. My mother had been waiting several years to be a grandmother and was so excited when Paris was born, and she formed a beautiful bond with her.

As my amazing girl grew up, each year going by so fast, I was so thankful for this precious child, she was the easiest child to raise, perhaps given she was fairly mature (like her mum). We formed an incredible bond from the moment she was placed in my arms and it grew from there, I knew somehow we were soulmates. I knew we had done this before, this mother and daughter thing, although it felt at times she had been my mother and I was the daughter.

(It was years later that I was told this exact thing by a few psychics, and when I fully excelled at tapping into my wisdom and soul records, amongst other things, I saw for myself this was the case. Our bond as mother and daughter was so close, and we often come to earth together in support of each other, we have had many lives together)

I knew the way I was 'given' her name it was prearranged, a sign that we both were being guided, as it was quite interesting. I was standing in a line at the mall one day and a lady with a toddler was in front of me, she turned around to speak to her child and called her Paris. In that instant it was like a light went off in me and I thought that's it, that's her name. The next day, my brother rang me from overseas to tell me that he had heard this beautiful name for a girl, and thought I should call our baby this if I had a girl. I asked him what the name was and he said, "Paris." I couldn't believe it, *or maybe I could*, I knew it was synchronicity from the universe and that was the name they had chosen for her. It helped that I was in love with the name and so was my husband, so for us there was no question.

***

I had 16 years with my lovely husband, the two of us venturing together, but it was time now to say goodbye. We had been through so many triumphs and tragedies as one does in life, but as difficult as these times can be, we remained very good friends, which kept it easy for our girl. Divorce is never easy and all the adjustment period was hard on all of us, but as time passed by it showed me I had made the correct decision. I had spent too many years without myself, and it was time to try and find ME again.

So after my divorce, I desired to search deeper into myself, a journey I had dismissed several times in my life, despite the universe and my beautiful love energy showing me. I dismissed it out of fear, self-judgment, other's judgment of me, being a somewhat 'people pleaser', fearing being different to others, *instead of celebrating the difference* because who wanted to be the same.

Still, I followed the rules and now the rules were set to be broken. (As rules are meant to be) It was time to explore within, so I started searching to find that connection back to myself, who I really was. (And I learnt it's not an overnight job that's for sure- well not for me it wasn't) However as much as I had lots of fun, adventures, stood stronger as an independent woman in all areas, I can't say there was much time to really go within and explore my spirituality. I had felt I was getting closer to my roots though. I took up yoga weekly, studied energy a little, built my house around Feng Shui, but didn't really have time to step into my full metaphysical gifts, (in a way I still doubted many things) but when you're a single mum as most single mums know, there isn't a lot of time left for yourself, but I didn't mind so much because I felt blessed to have my daughter, and she was my priority.

Being a parent is not easy, but I thought the one way I could be a good parent in my eyes, was to always instil the power of love, trust, forgiveness, truth and understanding, and if I could do this than I was on my way to being a successful parent, and hopefully have a beautiful trusting relationship with my daughter… And I did.

Chapter 24
Stay with Me

It was 2008 – I was 41, *where had those years gone*, and it was now five years since my divorce. I was still single and not a great deal had changed in terms of delving further into my spirituality, or finding that hidden mystery of what my purpose was, or why 'all those years ago' I was told to stay. Some days I would look back on my life and think – I never thought it would work out like this – and at 41, I had still not found what it was I'm here to do. Those words when I was 16, I had never shared with a soul, that day my energy friend saved my life, it was just him, and I that knew. I had carried that secret of the events that day with me, so deeply in my heart. It was something we shared together. All these years on I still remembered, as life moves on there are many things we forget, but never did I forget his words and his voice so vividly, it was something I could never forget. In lots of ways, it still felt like it was yesterday to me. But as I would flash back to those times, those decades of growing up with him, in some ways it was too painful to recall, because I missed him so – and after all my asking he was still not with me in human form. So because of this a large part of me had now given up looking for what it was I was here for.

I had built a lovely home for Paris and I, and we had been comfortably living there for four years. She had grown up into the most beautiful teenager with so much love, compassion, and kindness to share; she respected herself and believed in her unique choices and ability to be herself. (Something her mum never had the courage to show) But I could see she too, had her struggles with the way this world was, just like her mother did. I had remembered my struggles, they were still silent, hidden beneath for no one to see, but I remembered. So I made sure I helped her navigate her path to the best I could, hoping she could have it a little easier than me. I brought a great deal of awareness into her life, and I listened to her and allowed when she was using her incredible gifts and intuition. I made sure she felt completely comfortable to do so, and to be her true self. We were still living in a world, *believe it or not,* similar to when I grew up. There was not a great deal of conscious people around, or living and expressing their life from a spiritual aspect. In many ways, it had become more materialistic and fast pace with many living deeper within the matrix (our conditioned paradigm). And most living and making choices from fear.

My life was relatively ordinary, and I was living the daily life of a single mum whilst trying to keep it all together, mortgage, bills, trying to help others where I could, and hope I would have a little time left over for me at the end of the week. At this particular time, I was suffering some trauma from the year before, and I had been diagnosed with Post Traumatic Stress Disorder, but I was trying hard to get back on my feet. However, waking up each day and moving forward, to be honest, was all I could manage and was praying for. Life at this time was difficult for me, and those that have had PTSD would understand. PTSD can also bring with it 'those suicidal thoughts' but this time my life was different, I had Paris – and there is no doubt in my mind she is what kept me from going to those places. But I admit, I had those thoughts again. I knew if somehow I could get through each day, I would find the strength inside me to keep going, as I had already done over the many traumas throughout my life to date. I was still that little girl inside, I shut down and shared very little, going within, being the *silent introvert.* Some close friends had a deeper understanding of how I felt more than others, as I showed very little on the outside, but still inside I was dying.

However, I was about to see the universe would grant me the most amazing prayer of all, and I could see the timing perfectly. Out of nowhere the most extraordinary occurred.

One Friday night, in the early hours of the evening, there was a knock at my door. I was expecting someone, as through a chain of events where I was helping a friend, I knew they were coming. But what I didn't know was, I was to see this was actually for me, sent to me from the universe, and sent to change my life.

As my door opened I looked up to see a young man standing before me, and as he looked back at me and our eyes locked, an incredible jolt shuddered through my body, like a surge of pure energy and recognition. It felt a bit like an explosion within me. His face, those eyes, his appearance, I had seen before, and his incredible energy I had felt...and then he spoke... His voice shook me to my core, and I knew I had heard it before, everything about him was familiar. I knew him, yet we had never met. I had heard his voice, yet we had never spoken. I'd felt his energy, yet I had never been around him. I was paralyzed, in shock, and in that moment I had no clue what I was saying or doing. Time stood still, and I felt like I was walking around in my body, but not actually connected to it, like I was somewhere else.

My mind was asking how I knew him. The feeling was surreal. I tried to look away so he didn't think I was staring, but my eyes felt bonded to his, it was like a resonance within me I'd known before. I felt I had to cover up my weirdness or the way I felt in case he did not recognize me, maybe it was just me, and he didn't remember me at all, so I had to act normal, but normal was definitely something I couldn't do or be that night. When I looked into his eyes, I could see through into his soul, and when he looked back at me, I felt he could see through into mine. At times, when I was trying hard to not lock eyes or look his way, I couldn't help myself, and I would glance over to see he would be doing the same thing, looking back at me. Did this mean he felt something too? Did he feel what I felt or anything similar? Was I familiar to him? Did he remember me? Did he know what was happening between us? I couldn't be sure, but *my* heart and *his* energy was telling me he did. And I could clearly feel that he felt a connection to me, like I did him. To what degree I had no idea, but I knew how I felt, and my soul felt like it had unlocked inside of me taking me to a different place.

Each time he spoke, his voice hit me like a lightning bolt, recognition of his voice I could not place but remember, and it flowed with a vibration that triggered my heart open. My mind trying to analyze from logic but something else here was definitely more powerful. My heart and soul was at the forefront and as bizarre as it sounds, I felt it was a dreamlike state, something beyond this existence.

Words escaped me as he spoke to others. My head was in one place but everything else was in another. Something so incredibly unique was occurring here, and I felt exposed – fully in that moment, but yet such incredible relief, like something was aligning perfectly. It didn't feel scary or weird; it felt entirely perfect. He felt entirely perfect. An angel had just entered my home, his pure angelic energy presence was undeniable the energy I had felt before, but where, and how did we know each other.

I could actually feel him saying "I know her", he was feeling something about me that was very familiar to him to, but he was most likely just as confused as me. We had an instant connection, and I was mesmerized. To me, it felt like we were joined in some way, but I couldn't figure how, there was also this overwhelming feeling that he belonged in my home and should stay.

(When I was little, and throughout my younger life, my energy friend walked with me, stayed with me, protected me, and was always there even when I closed off from him. He was always there guiding and taking care of me. The only one I felt close enough to be myself with, talk from my heart, the one that knew me completely, the real me, the one that stopped me from taking my life with his words in my bedroom that fateful day, the one that was my love. The love I felt so different to any other, that euphoric love that felt so unlike earth love or what others seemed to have.)

This magical supernatural experience I was repeating could only mean one thing. Was it HIM? In human form? My beautiful love, was he really here? Was he listening to me asking after all? Was the universe listening to me asking, asking him to 'please come be with me' and did he know he was coming? He knew he was coming, he told me that day, "I'm coming." He knew, and here he was. It was so hard to believe it was real, but there was no mistaking that energy, I could never mistake his energy… After all these years – my whole life – he had finally walked into my life in human form. I had waited 41 years for him to come be with me, and here he was standing next to me as a physical being. However the circumstances he came to be in my home was not to see me, so I couldn't say anything. So once again, I kept it silent. But what I was feeling was incredibly surreal and so magical. It felt like a miracle beyond a miracle. To actually have this become a reality, and for him and the universe to be correct in all they told me and guided me with my entire life, it was just beyond mind blowing. After he left that night I didn't know what to do or think, but he had obviously felt a remembrance of me and our energy, because he contacted me and asked to see me, just us two, on our own.

Our first night alone together was the most extraordinary night of my life. We talked and in those hours it felt like time did really stand still. The outside world didn't exist. It was just us, and my thoughts were never away from us. I had never experienced this before; we hear about it but rarely see it. To me it was like we were the only ones that existed. And everything felt completely aligned. I knew the time was coming where he would touch me, and we would be intimate, my heart was pounding and that little girl nervousness was shaking inside. To have all you have asked for your whole life to be before your eyes was magical but a little scary at the same time. I wanted to be everything he expected from me, but I didn't know what that was. Sitting on my sofa he was so relaxed, carefree, and looked like he was in a total state of bliss, he was an angel to me, he was my angel, but my ego was working overtime telling me 'I was no angel' and would I disappoint him. My heart was at the forefront and was not going to let those thoughts when the time came, overshadow our experience. When he touched me, I opened to his full magnificence and power that he brought to us, when his hands touched my skin it felt electric and my entire body was awakened. I was still unsure of what was happening between us, but when we held each other, touched each other, embraced our bodies so intimately together, it was pure magic. He took over holding me in his arms, as I surrendered to him completely, there was no denying our connection or the way we worked, it just happened automatically, and it felt so perfect. He was the one to take charge, like he had always done with us through the years, but this time he was in physical form and we saw together, how it worked so perfectly. My beloved energy friend, his beauty before me, I was astounded in his presence. Still not being able to comprehend exactly what we were to each other, but it didn't matter, all I knew was something so magical was happening that night, and it would be a night I would never forget.

As our night came to a close and he stood at my bedroom door saying goodbye, every part of me desired from an inner strength and power, to reach out and say to him:

"Stay with me, please don't leave, stay with me."

I had asked him for years to "Please come be with me", and now he was finally here I wanted to ask him to

"Please stay with me."

But before I knew it, he was halfway down my stairs and walking out my front door, and as I heard that front door shut, I felt he had taken half of me with him. I realized in that moment he was *always* my missing piece.

I never knew how my love would enter my life, or when, but from a little girl I knew he would. I knew I would have that love. I tried so many times to call him in, to manifest him with me in physical form. I knew he was coming, every part of me knew he was meant to be here with me, but I didn't know when. (And yes at times I gave up.)

You see we always know we are connected to something, but where is it? Who is it? What is it? We may find it in the strangest places or unique situations, it may come to us so unexpected, but the truth is, if it's meant to be, it will always find a way. This time as my beautiful 'human' divine soul partner he had found me. He had found me in this *small little town* I still lived in, the one I never imagined I would find my true love. The universe had even brought us together in the *same little township*, can you believe out of the entire world they brought him to me, here!

He had walked with me as I took the first part of my life, helping me fly through life, with his wings, now with our amazing universe intervening, he had found me, as soon as he was old enough, and now our journey in the physical had begun.

Maybe not everyone will find 'The One' in this lifetime, or is meant too. Not all may meet their soulmate or one soul connection. But one things for sure, for those of us who just know inside that we will, trust that, trust what you feel, trust in the universe and its infinite power, because it's beyond magical. After traveling together through my youth, waiting for him to travel through his, I had found my true love, we had again 'found each other' but this time both in human form. We were now both journeying in this world together, now both...*flying without wings.*

END

I owe it to the universe, energy, and the power of love.

www.ingramcontent.com/pod-product-compliance
Lightning Source LLC
Chambersburg PA
CBHW060825050426
42453CB00008B/588